The
BEST ANSWER

9 Secrets of
Job-Winning
Interviews

DEB GOTTESMAN AND BUZZ MAURO

B
BERKLEY BOOKS, NEW YORK

THE BERKLEY PUBLISHING GROUP
Published by the Penguin Group
Penguin Group (USA) Inc.
375 Hudson Street, New York, New York 10014, USA
Penguin Group (Canada), 90 Eglinton Avenue East, Suite 700, Toronto, Ontario M4P 2Y3, Canada (a division of Pearson Penguin Canada Inc.)
Penguin Books Ltd., 80 Strand, London WC2R 0RL, England
Penguin Group Ireland, 25 St. Stephen's Green, Dublin 2, Ireland (a division of Penguin Books Ltd.)
Penguin Group (Australia), 250 Camberwell Road, Camberwell, Victoria 3124, Australia (a division of Pearson Australia Group Pty. Ltd.)
Penguin Books India Pvt. Ltd., 11 Community Centre, Panchsheel Park, New Delhi—110 017, India
Penguin Group (NZ), Cnr. Airborne and Rosedale Roads, Albany, Auckland 1310, New Zealand (a division of Pearson New Zealand Ltd.)
Penguin Books (South Africa) (Pty.) Ltd., 24 Sturdee Avenue, Rosebank, Johannesburg 2196, South Africa

Penguin Books Ltd., Registered Offices: 80 Strand, London WC2R 0RL, England

While the author has made every effort to provide accurate telephone numbers and Internet addresses at the time of publication, neither the publisher nor the author assumes any responsibility for errors, or for changes that occur after publication. The publisher does not have any control over and does not assume any responsibility for author or third-party websites or their content.

PRINTING HISTORY
Berkley trade paperback edition: April 2006

Library of Congress Cataloging-in-Publication Data

Gottesman, Deb.
   The best answer : 9 secrets of job-winning interviews / Deb Gottesman and Buzz Mauro.—1st ed.
      p. cm.
   ISBN 0-425-20793-5
      1. Employment interviewing. I. Title: Nine secrets of job-winning interviews.
   II. Mauro, Buzz. III. Title.

HF5549.5.I6G68 2006
650.14'4—dc22   2005055317

PRINTED IN THE UNITED STATES OF AMERICA

10 9 8 7 6 5 4 3 2 1

The
BEST ANSWER

ONTENTS

Part Four

A Personal Note from the Authors

CALL US CRAZY, but we don't think job interviews should drive people crazy.

A few years ago we published a comprehensive job interview manual called *The Interview Rehearsal Book*. It shows readers how to use acting techniques to give a confident, authentic, job-winning interview performance, and we believe that its considerable success has been due to its easy-to-master, common-sense approach.

But since that time, something strange and terrible has happened in the ever-expanding American job search industry: Suddenly everyone seems to think it's possible—and desirable—to prepare ahead of time for *every conceivable* interview question. Job interview candidates across the country are carrying around lists of hundreds of different questions that might get asked—and *memorizing* the answers they're told are the right ones!

We firmly believe that these lists are a waste of time, for a variety of reasons that we'll explain in this book. The main reason, though, is that the best answer to any job interview question must be unique to *you*, so you're clearly not going to find it on someone else's list.

In the time since we wrote *The Interview Rehearsal Book*, we've come to see that this issue of how to answer the questions deserves a more detailed examination than we gave it in that book, and that's why we've written this one. (*The Interview Rehearsal Book* covers all aspects of self-presentation in the job interview, with just a short section on the mechanics of questions and answers. We urge you to read it as part of your overall interview training, but it's certainly not a prerequisite for understanding the techniques presented here.)

The book you hold in your hands is designed to stop the madness. It will show you how it's possible to do a terrific interview without struggling through hundreds of pages and memorizing hundreds of answers. It will prepare you for 1,000,001 interview questions—and more!—by training you in the elements of the best answer to *any possible question*. You already possess everything you need to do your best in any interview: *yourself*, with all your unique traits, experiences and accomplishments. This book will show you how to offer all that to an employer in the way that makes you most hireable, no matter what questions he or she decides to ask. We hope it will take some of the pressure off and free you up to give your best possible interview—and, ultimately, land the job you're looking for without driving yourself crazy in the process.

Deb Gottesman and Buzz Mauro

PART 1

The Only Useful Way to Approach a Job Interview

PEOPLE WORRY ABOUT all the wrong things in life. They worry they don't have a nice enough car to keep up with their neighbors. They faint at the sight of a gray hair. They're apoplectic that their son or daughter might not get into Harvard, as if any other school on the face of the planet would be a blot on the family name.

And although we'd all like to think otherwise, it's a sad fact that *very* few of us are completely immune. Worrying is part of human nature. It's there to nag us into remembering to protect ourselves when the going gets dicey. Cavemen must have worried about being eaten by beasts, and worrying was probably a good thing for them. Those who didn't give a hoot did not survive to pass their devil-may-care genes down to us moderns.

But nowadays, people's worries often center on significantly less serious threats. Like the threat of embarrassment or of exceeding their daily carb limit. Or of being considered old, unattractive, geeky or otherwise dispensable to a society that's often perceived as hostile, even though the saber-toothed tigers aren't much of a problem anymore.

And when you step out into the unfamiliar terrain of the job market, these peculiarly modern worries spread like poison ivy. *What if they ask me a question I can't answer? What if I get nervous and my hands start to shake? What if I inadvertently insult the interviewer? What if I spill coffee in my lap? What if I make a complete fool of myself? What if they see right through me?*

Job interview worries are perhaps more justifiable than some, because the search for a job is really about securing certain fundamental necessities that even the cavemen would have appreciated, like food, shelter and a decent pair of jeans.

But if you look a little closer at the typical interview anxieties, you'll see that very few are worth the mental energy it takes to think them up. They arise from our almost (but not quite) inescapable human need to anticipate the worst. And there are plenty of people out there just waiting to capitalize on your fears. Unscrupulous career coaches will tell you that the only way to prepare for a job interview is to memorize hundreds of specific interview questions and painstakingly prepare your answer to each. And they just happen to have the inside info you're looking for: the exact list of questions and, oh look! a handy crib sheet that will get you an A every time. Each and every one of those questions is a land mine, buddy, but if you invest the right amount of time (hundreds of hours) and money (God only knows how much), these charlatans will do their best to help you avoid the catastrophe that's awaiting you.

Nonsense. The truth is that many of the things job candidates worry about are not serious threats at all. Many are just plain silly, in fact, and the best way to start your interview preparation is by crossing them off your list. Delete them from your worry bank before going any further, because *they are not going to happen*. You will not trip over the carpet on your way in and fall flat on your face. You will not disgust the interviewer with the sweatiness of your handshake. The interviewer will not secretly laugh at the inadequacy of your experience. Just face these facts right off the bat. It's thinking awfully highly of yourself to assume that your interview will be especially memorable in any way without any special effort on your part. You will either distinguish yourself as a finalist for the position, or you won't.

Of course, some of the worries people bring into the interview are less silly. Yes, some of the bad things people spend so much time dreaming up might actually, just maybe, happen, but even most of those are not really so terrible. It's possible, for example, that someone else who's applying for the job may look a lot better than you on paper. (But you got in the door anyway, so they can't have looked *that* much better.) It's possible that as you leave the room you'll realize you failed to tell your best story, even though you had the perfect opportunity to do so. (But your interviewer didn't know which stories you were going to tell, so whatever stories you *did* tell probably sufficed.) It's possible that you will find the interviewer hard to talk to. (And so will everyone else in the world.)

The critical point—which we all know but often forget to remember—is that worrying about these potential problems will not solve them. For one thing, they're not real problems, just potential ones, so solving them is not even really an option. But even though it's within the realm of possibility that any of these things could happen, and therefore they might be considered worthy of worrying about, two major points distinguish them from a prehistoric saber-toothed attack: 1) the probability of their actually occurring is low, and 2) if they did occur, it wouldn't be as awful as we (for some reason) like to think. Thus, worry is the wrong approach.

The right approach is to focus not on the bad things that might happen, but on a few techniques and strategies that will maximize the likelihood that something good will happen—like a job offer. The best way to avoid tripping while walking down the sidewalk is not to maintain a worried concentration on all possible tripping hazards, but to focus on the goal of getting to the next corner. Too intent a focus on the cracks in the sidewalk is unlikely to do anything but make you lose your balance. If you focus on what's most important about the whole walking business, the balancing part takes care of itself.

This book will prepare you for 1,000,001 job interview questions by detailing the characteristics of the best answer to any possible question, and training you to focus on all the right things. We'll use specific questions as examples, but always as a way of explaining principles that apply across the board. Once you have the principles under your belt, there will be no need to memorize hundreds of specific situations, because you will be prepared for anything and everything.

We once heard a fellow interview coach give the following "tip" to a roomful of job candidates. He said that if you're worried about being nervous, you should be sure to bring a rubber band to the interview. Keep it in your pocket and stretch it and play with it throughout the interview as a way to dissipate nervous energy. Problem solved!

Personally, we're not big on little "tips" of this nature. We're bigger on *training*, and you'll get lots of that in the upcoming pages. But anything that calls itself a "tip" tends to sound very practical and yet have limited actual value in the real world. The rubber band thing may even be actively detrimental to the quality of an interview.

By all means, feel free to try it if you like—but don't you think it might *exacerbate* your nerves, rather than alleviate them? It could very easily make you *focus on your nervousness* throughout the interview! It's a bit like tying a string around your finger to make sure you never forget how nervous you are. To us, that sounds like a bad idea. Whatever nervous energy gets dissipated into the rubber band is sure to return with a vengeance because of where you've placed your focus.

The ideas and techniques we'll present in this book are designed to get your focus off potential problems and onto potential successes. When we talk about the need to be truthful, we won't focus on what a dangerous trap lying is, but on how truthfulness actually opens up possibilities for you. When we say an answer should not be too long, we won't let you get paranoid about going over a time limit; we'll help you learn to use conciseness to your advantage.

Like most things in life, interview success has a lot to do with how you view the process. See it as a burden and it will be—to both you and your interviewer. See it as a chance to celebrate what you have to offer and you'll give someone else a reason to see it that way, too.

The Myth of the Right Answer

A few years ago we worked with a job candidate (we'll call him Frank) who was back in the job market for the first time in twenty-seven years, after being downsized out of the company he had planned to be with for the rest of his working life. Frank was understandably a pretty depressed guy. He felt very out of touch with the current job market and was afraid he was too old to get a good job. Someone had referred him to us. Apparently he came only out of desperation, and not really believing that anything could help him.

He spent his time with us asking lots of questions about how job searches and interviews were being done "these days." He wanted to know all about the current tricks of the trade, what kind of questioning was popular at the moment, what employers were looking for, etc. To a small extent we were able to fill him in on current trends, but we emphasized that that was exactly what they were: just trends. And the thing about a trend is that it's a gross generalization about how people are doing things. Who are these "people," anyway? They're a bunch of individuals, some of whom pay lots of attention to trends and some of whom don't. He was looking for a magic key, like, "Tell them you're a team player and you'll have it made."

If there were such a thing as a magic key to the corporate door, we would have gladly given it to him. But, of course, it doesn't exist. If the "team player" line is being used frequently enough to become a trend, it's also being used frequently enough to become a cliché. Or worse: a cop-out. A pathetic attempt to go where the crowd seems to be leading.

To get Frank out of his unproductive way of thinking, we put him in some mock interview situations, where he would have to practice answering questions without being given time to prepare some kind of ideal answer ahead of time. (Since you have no way of knowing what questions will really get asked, this is the way interviews actually work.) His interview skills turned out to be among the worst we've ever witnessed. He was practically paralyzed with fear. He seemed defensive, even hostile, and was unable to show us any reason why someone might want to work with him. We tried everything we could think of to calm him down and loosen him up, to very little avail.

Eventually one of us said, almost offhandedly, "You know, Frank, the interviewer is not sitting there with the correct answer in his head, waiting to see if you'll get it right or wrong."

He looked at us as if we'd spoken Chinese. And then he said, "He's not? What's the point of the interview then?"

The idea that the interview is nothing but a test was deeply ingrained in Frank's way of thinking about the whole employer/employee dynamic. *They know the answers, and my job is to guess them. If I pass the test, then I may get hired. If I fail, then I lose, they win and I'm on the bread line.*

Once we finally convinced him that the point of interviews is not to determine which job candidate can answer the most questions correctly, a wonderful thing happened. He started talking. Far from confidently at first, but at least he was talking. And eventually he got around to saying some things that showed us how he was able to be highly successful at his previous job for twenty-seven years.

Frank's answers were not full of buzzwords and up-to-date jargon, and it was only by giving up on the idea that those things were important—that the questions had to be answered in some very particular way or they would be "wrong"—that he was able to impress us with things that matter so much more, like what he had accomplished in the past and hoped to accomplish in the future.

This idea that there's a right answer in the interviewer's mind for each question and that she's testing you to see how many you'll miss, is probably the most insidious and harmful of the many myths about how job interviews work. Recently it's led to a kind of mass hysteria that has people thinking they need to know the answer to every possible question before the interview begins. But let's face facts: besides being wrong-headed, that goal is simply *impossible*.

It's no mystery why people reach for a book that claims to provide all the answers. It's certainly comforting to be told that the best answer to "What's your greatest weakness?" is, "I'm a workaholic." No more thinking or worrying required! But even if it were possible to memorize the answer to every possible question, the interviewers you're going to face out there are not stupid. They're catching on. If you give them the "workaholic" answer, they'll know you've read it in a book and they'll draw the obvious conclusion that you don't have enough creativity, self-confidence or honesty to come up with a truthful, thoughtful answer of your own.

We're here to help you come up with those truthful, thoughtful answers by training you to focus on the right things both before and during your interview. With the right focus and an accurate understanding of how job interviews really work, you'll be prepared to answer *any* question that may come your way. And your answers will both reflect the truth of who you are and maximize your chances of getting the job.

The truth is, the interviewer has a problem—she needs to fill a position at her company—and she would like nothing more than for you to be the solution. That means she needs to find out who *you* are. She has no use for canned answers. And she's not interested in weeding you out, but in giving you every chance to show that you're the one who can solve her problem for her by being the right person for the job. The questions are her way of helping you talk about yourself in ways that might help her make that decision. So if you want to give the best possible answers, you start by thinking of each question as an *opportunity*.

A Land of Opportunity

If the interview is your opportunity to show who you are and why you should be hired—and that's exactly what it is—then, like any opportunity, it's up to you to take full advantage of it, squander it or do something in between. Ultimately, you *choose* how you use the interview opportunity. You may think you're a powerless pawn in the whole process, but if you allow that attitude to dominate, you're doomed before you walk into the room.

There's nothing predetermined about how the interview will go. Sometimes people seem to think it's all up to the interviewer—he will either magically understand exactly what you're all about or else get you completely wrong, compare you to his impression of the other candidates and then hand down some arbitrary, biased opinion. But that opinion is based not on who you really are or on some figment of the interviewer's imagination, but on the specific parts of you you've chosen to let the interviewer see.

And the biggest mistake interviewees make is to let the interviewer see too little. Some do it by preparing what they think are the "correct" answers ahead of time, thereby hiding their true selves. But more often, job candidates simply trust that the process will take care of itself—*he'll ask questions and I'll answer them, and that'll be it*—and many an interview opportunity thus disappears down the drain. Because answering in whatever way seems "natural" or "spontaneous" to you at the moment is most often not enough to do the trick. Such a *que sera, sera* attitude will probably lead to a bunch of answers that feel truthful and pertinent, but don't go nearly far enough in letting the interviewer understand who you are and what you can do.

We wish we could tell you that Frank overcame his interviewing problems and went on to a fantastic career in his chosen field. But we can't tell you what Frank's future had in store for him, because we never heard from him again. As you can see, though, we haven't forgotten him. He represents all the interviewees out there with the potential to be debilitated by the misconception that who they really are is somehow not enough. Our hope is that he eventually convinced himself of the silliness of that attitude and learned to treat the interview as an opportunity rather than an interrogation. And even if he didn't, we can still have that hope for you.

The rest of this book will show you the right way to prepare for a job interview: Learn to ignore all the distracting nonsense that often gets in the way and focus on a few tested techniques for showing who you are and why you're right for the job, no matter what questions happen to be asked.

Here's what you can expect to get from this book:

- A systematic process for finding the best way to answer *any* interview question

- Training in using your unique qualities, rather than formulaic answers, to impress any interviewer

- The truth about what interviewers are really looking for and ideas for helping you address the interviewer's needs

- A new, more relaxed outlook based on the fact that there is no single correct answer to any given question

- Relief from the anxiety of wondering which questions will be asked, because you'll be prepared for anything

- Preparation for succeeding not only in the interview but on the job as well, because by the end of the book you will have clearly envisioned and articulated why you are the right match for the position.

PART 2

The Worst Answer

OKAY, LET'S GET THIS out of the way first.

There's only one interview pitfall that we think is a serious enough threat that worrying about it a little might not be a bad idea. It happens all the time, job candidates frequently don't know it's happening and employers never fail to see it as a wasted opportunity. It's the empty answer. And it's coming soon to a workplace near you.

The Empty Answer

An empty answer is, by definition, one that lacks substance. It provides the interviewer with no memorable insights into the potential of the interviewee and thereby fails to advance the interview conversation. It generally happens when candidates take the path of least resistance, surrendering all control to the interviewer and answering the questions minimally, flatly—sometimes even dutifully.

This kind of answer is much worse—and much easier to perpetrate, because it requires practically no effort—than almost any potential gaffe. (We'll assume throughout this book that you're a basically sensible person who is unlikely to blurt out a desire to decapitate the interviewer or something. That would be worse.)

No single empty answer will sink an interview, but a series of them will add up to one big wasted opportunity, and the need to line up another interview pronto. The good news is that with preparation and alertness, the problem is easy to fix, and we've got lots of strategies for doing just that. But first you need to thoroughly understand what it is you're trying to avoid, so have a look at what's next.

The empty answer comes in many forms, all of them insidious.

THE CLASSIC "YES" OR "NO"

Simple, direct and assured. But what a waste.

A good interviewer will avoid asking yes-or-no questions, precisely because they tend to produce yes-or-no answers, which provide very little bang for the interviewer's buck. Fun as the game of Twenty Questions can be, it can take an awful long time to figure out what's what when all you get is a series of affirmatives and negatives. Much better for everyone if the interview is less of a puzzle.

So good interviewers don't ask very many yes-or-no questions, but less seasoned ones do, and when it happens, it's up to you to create opportunity. If your interviewer asks, "So, do you have much experience managing a large team?"—this is technically a yes-or-no question, and with the stress of the interview situation you may be sorely tempted to do your duty by providing the required monosyllable and leave it at that. But a yes-or-no answer would be ludicrous here. It would be a blunt impediment to the flow of conversation, for one thing, but also a wasted opportunity to share specifics of your talents and experiences that would set you apart from the competition. We don't believe there are many hard-and-fast rules in the world of job interviewing, but here's one to get you started: *Never answer "Yes" or "No" without elaborating.*

The best way to elaborate is usually by giving an example. We'll show you how in the next chapter.

THE VAGUE EVASION

Not all monosyllables are created equal, of course. If your interviewer asks you if you've ever managed a large group, a simple "Yes" is not very good, but "No" is certainly worse.

It's a very small pool of especially inept interviewees who would ever baldly answer "No" to that and then calmly await the next question. But the following almost-as-empty answers are typical of the kind of evasions this situation can inspire:

"Not really, but I was next in line for team leader last year. Some young guy from another division got the position instead."

"We actually had really big team units at my last job. My supervisor always gave me the highest possible scores for efficiency and courteousness."

"Define 'large' for me."

Even if the technically correct answer to this question is "No," it's an opportunity to segue into *something* about your experience and qualifications that might make the interviewer think you're prepared to manage a large team. Evading any question wastes the opportunity, and also makes you seem shifty and unreliable. (Interviewers generally remember what question they asked, and they're likely to notice if you fail to answer it.) Instead, you should interpret the question in a way that allows you to give the interviewer some usable information. Something like, "Well, at my last job we worked in pretty small teams, but I learned a lot about managing larger groups when I headed up my PTA's standards committee. . . ." We'll give special consideration to this idea later, when we address "the question behind the question."

RÉSUMÉ REGURGITATION

"What kind of sales experience do you have?"

"For the last seven years I was head of sales at the McCarthy Stationery Company in St. Louis, Missouri."

Chances are good that your interviewer can read. So please don't simply repeat what your résumé has already told him. Since he has the piece of paper in his possession, repetition of what it says constitutes an empty answer. The interview is your opportunity to go beyond the raw facts. Even if you suspect that he hasn't read your résumé as thoroughly as you would like, or if he seems to have forgotten some of the details, a simple reminder is not a very good use of your time. Instead, remind and expand:

"As head of sales at McCarthy Stationery, I increased revenue by 23 percent in the seven years I was there, and learned a lot about recent trends in sales techniques." Something true and specific, of course, but something that takes your résumé and runs with it.

You'll find lots of practical advice for getting off the page in the upcoming chapters.

THE "I DON'T KNOW"

There's nothing wrong with admitting that you don't know something. If the interviewer asks you, "How big is the budget of the last company you worked for?" and you don't know the answer, you certainly should not pull a number out of thin air. Feel free to admit that you don't know, but please go on to give a good explanation of why that was not important to the job that you did there, and perhaps let the interviewer know that you'd be happy to find that information out if he really wants to know.

It's best, though, not to admit ignorance of something that is central to your qualifications for the job in question. For example, if asked, "What are your qualifications for this job?"—please don't say, "Come to think of it, I don't really know." The same goes for, "Why did you leave your last position?" or, "What makes you want to work for us?" or anything else that directly addresses your experience and qualifications. It's your job to know these things and to be prepared to explain, but we'll help you find ways of using what you know to your best advantage.

IDLE CHATTER

One kind of empty answer suffers not from being too short, but from being too long. It's just as empty as the other kinds, but this one is empty at length.

We're talking about irrelevant chatter, chitchat, banter, small talk and shooting the breeze. If you're applying for a job as an elementary school music teacher, for instance, the strongest answer to "Do you have any hobbies?" is not "Yes," but it's also not "Oh my god. I am a major philatelist. I got started when my brother and I were kids on the farm in Nebraska. I have three rare Federal Duck Stamps and a super-rare 13-cent Liberty Bell Imperforate Error. I've been on the lookout for a mint condition 24-cent Curtis Jenny for years, so if you hear of a dealer who may have one, please let me know ASAP. I also love most forms of fly-fishing and making my own taffy, of course—in fact I'd love to share a favorite recipe with you."

It's easy (easier than you may think) to fall into this kind of substanceless, chatty answer when you're nervous. Some people even do it intentionally, thinking that adding a lot of personal detail helps in establishing rapport. It's dangerous, though, because too much chatter both makes you seem unprofessional and wastes precious interview time that could be used to position yourself as the must-have candidate. You'll only do it, though, if you're not ready to catch yourself at it, or if you haven't prepared a better approach.

For the aspiring music teacher, a brief statement about his music-related side interests (playing bass in a jazz group) or his work with kids (even if it's just pulling taffy with his nieces and nephews) will help advance the conversation far more than irrelevant talk of stamp collecting or anything else. And such relevant answers will come naturally if he has prepared appropriately by considering how his various interests and abilities might intersect with the needs of the position at hand.

Bringing Out the Worst in Us

It's important to recognize these various kinds of empty answers so you can catch yourself if you start to give them in the interview or—even better—steer completely clear of them. It's also important, though, to understand *why* so many people give empty answers in interviews. Understanding the psychology underlying the worst answers will allow you to change the interview dynamic in your favor. And only by doing that can you open yourself up to the best answers you have to give.

PLAYING DEFENSE

Like poor Frank from the last chapter, an awful lot of people seem to think the interviewer is the enemy, to be guarded against, outmaneuvered and—ideally—defeated (before he can defeat you).

We once interviewed someone—we'll call her Kate, because that was her name—for a coaching position. We already knew her professionally and had always found her to be smart, pleasant, creative and pretty much exactly what we were looking for in a candidate to fill the job. But when she walked in for the formal interview, it was as if she had become a completely different person. Unfortunately, this new person was sullen, terse, almost sarcastic. Luckily for her, we knew her well enough to surmise that this unpleasant front was just a defensive reaction to the stress of the interview situation and we cut her some slack. We hired her based on what we already knew of her, and she turned out to be a terrific employee. But if that interview had been our introduction to her, she wouldn't have stood a chance.

That kind of defensiveness is one of those fight-or-flight mechanisms that can kick in when things get stressful. It arises from the fear of being wrong, or of making a bad impression, or of being powerless, or of job interviews in general. The only way to avoid it is, first, to be on the lookout for it, and second, to beat it into submission with logic: What in the world is there to defend against? The interviewer is not attacking you, for Pete's sake. She's asking you some questions, hoping maybe you'll be the right one for the job so she can go have lunch and relax. Putting up a wall of any kind is certainly going to be counterproductive.

The attitude you take with you into the interview is one of the easiest things for you to control, so why not turn the knob all the way to positive and see what happens? You'll be doing yourself a big favor.

RÉSUMÉ RELIANCE

This is the widespread belief that one's résumé speaks for itself. It doesn't.

People think it does, because that would be so nice. There it is: all the important stuff, already beautifully presented on a piece of high-quality bond. *Which means this interview thing is just a technicality, right? Guess I can relax and wing it.*

If your résumé spoke for itself, there wouldn't be a need for an interview at all, would there? Your résumé is a reference work: just the facts, no plot, no character, no suspense; none of the good stuff. Your résumé is a starting block. It got you in the race.

What you do when the gun sounds is what really matters.

EXCESSIVE POLITENESS

Politeness is good, but it is possible to overdo it. Bowing to the interviewer would be an example of that in our culture, as would insisting on warming up her coffee for her.

As would giving only the briefest of answers as a way of showing respect for the interviewer's time. Yes-or-no answers can seem extremely efficient and respectful, but if you want the job, you'll have to be a bit bolder than that. Take the leap and assume you're interesting enough to hold the interviewer's attention. Dare to take up some of her time. She's asked you there to do exactly that.

MEMORY MANIA

One of the worst kinds of empty answers comes from a belief that memorizing answers out of a book is somehow a good thing. That idea causes people to say their greatest weakness is being a perfectionist and their greatest strength is being a "go-getter" and other such nonsense.

By all means, learn *how* to give a great answer in an interview (by reading on), but please don't attempt to learn what answers to give. For one thing, you have no way of knowing what questions will be asked, so you'll have to do an awful lot of preparation that would end up being completely wasted. (That alone is plenty of reason not to spend a lot of time on "How would you move Mount Fuji?") But more important is the hollowness that characterizes all answers that someone else has told you are the "right" ones. They never ring true. They ring calculated, belabored, cliché and phony, and they tell the interviewer nothing unique about you. They're the ultimate waste of the interview opportunity.

WINGING IT

Most of us feel we know ourselves pretty well, and we're probably right. And that leads a lot of us to think there's no way to prepare for a job interview. The subject of the interview is *me*, and that's one of my favorite topics. What's to prepare?

Well, there are two main areas in which preparation is going to help a great deal. First, no matter how well you know yourself, it's a simple fact that a lot of things are going to fly out of your head during the interview unless you've done a little work ahead of time to make sure you remember them. So you'll do well to remind yourself of your good traits and sift through your memories to find the best possible illustrations of them so that your mind is not flailing around randomly when it's time to come up with the goods.

And second, it will help immeasurably to have a process for answering questions once you're in that room. Saying whatever comes into your head is a kind of process but it's not the one most likely to get you the job. Fortunately, there exist tools to help you answer interview questions to your best advantage, and a little practice in how to use them will make any interview a lot easier and a lot more effective.

The next section will explain how to prepare as efficiently and productively as possible.

PART 3

The Best Answer

HOLD ON A MINUTE. *The Best Answer?* If every answer to every interview question is supposed to be completely unique to you and to the job, then how can anyone tell you what's the best answer for *you* in any particular interview situation?

Good question. Glad you asked. To put it another way, we're not inside your head, so how can we help you express your unique uniqueness?

The reason we can have some helpful advice to offer is that the best answers to interview questions, although they're always specific to who's giving the answer (not to mention who's asking the question), do have certain characteristics in common. In fact, the best answers—the ones that make employers hire people—are surprisingly similar in many ways and across multiple interview situations. Your great answers are unique to you, of course. But they will necessarily share certain elements with all other great answers, just as a great movie can seem like a one-of-a-kind experience while you're enjoying it, but if looked at in-depth it will probably reveal a host of elements that are shared by most of the other movies you've enjoyed in your life: a pretty clear beginning-middle-end structure, a main character that you care about for some reason, a central conflict that is frustrating that character, and so on.

And that's the biggest secret we have to offer: All good answers are alike in certain very important ways. Having looked analytically at interview answers from lots of people in lots of interview situations over the course of lots of years, we've been able to identify nine elements that are crucial aspects of almost any good answer. And we've learned that job candidates who assimilate these nine elements—the secrets of what the best answers have in common—are pretty much prepared for any of the 1,000,001 interview questions that may come their way. These candidates don't have to prepare for specific individual questions or worry that the interviewer is going to throw them a curve they won't be able to handle. They know what makes an answer work, and that's all they need to know.

So here you go. These are the nine secrets of a good answer:

1. The Best Answer Is Truthful

2. The Best Answer Is Not Too Short

3. The Best Answer Is Not Too Long

4. The Best Answer Is Uniquely Yours

5. The Best Answer Paints a Picture of Who You Are

6. The Best Answer Demonstrates Knowledge of the Company

7. The Best Answer Addresses the Question Behind the Question

8. The Best Answer Is Active

9. The Best Answer Doesn't Have to Be the World's All-Time Best Answer

Seems pretty straightforward, but it all gets much more interesting when you put concepts like *truthful, unique* and *active* under the microscope and consider what they really mean in the interview situation. And that's where we have some valuable secrets to impart. So we'll now look at each of these characteristics in detail and show how you can use them to craft great answers that will get you the job by showing *you* in the best possible light.

Secret #1

The Best Answer Is Truthful

LET'S STATE THE OBVIOUS: Lying is bad. Bad for your soul (just like Mom told you) and bad for your job prospects. Employers do reference checks. People do a lot of chatting with other people in their industry. Word gets around, and people who misrepresent themselves lose their jobs and their reputations.

But we knew that already. Whether it's for ethical reasons or pragmatic ones, we can all agree that you should tell the truth in job interviews.

But what does that really mean? Should you divulge the details of your latest therapy session in the spirit of full disclosure? Should you tell your interviewer what you think of her hair to show how brutally honest you can be?

Of course not. To tell the truth, the whole truth and nothing but the truth makes perfect sense in the courtroom, but the job interview isn't a trial (no matter how much it may sometimes feel like one).

When interviewing for a job you certainly must tell the truth and nothing but the truth—but the *whole* truth is a different matter entirely.

After all, the whole truth about who you are is a pretty big subject. If you're a human being over the age of six months, you encompass a vast array of experiences, thoughts, attitudes, behaviors and more than a few contradictions. Perhaps you're a great listener, a lousy pianist, an engaging storyteller, a moderate snorer, an occasional overeater, an ambitious professional, a habitual procrastinator, a creative thinker, an anxious parent and, oh yeah, on your way here today you ran a yellow light. You can be naïve with your children and petty with your spouse and gossipy with your neighbor and snippy with your in-laws, as well as patient with your in-laws, trusting with your neighbor, romantic with your spouse and playful with your children.

But which of these truths belong in the job interview and which don't? And will the bald-faced truth really be enough to land you the job?

The Truth About Truth

One reason people are tempted to stretch the truth in job interviews is that they trust in their ability to do the job, but not in their ability to impress the employer enough to *get* the job. They know that if they can just get in the door, they'll be great, but lack of confidence in their interview skills leads them to believe that they're not going to get that far unless they "exaggerate" a tad. Luckily, it's possible to get the attention and respect of just about any employer without stooping to an ounce of prevarication.

The key to success is to *make smart decisions about which truths to tell.*

This takes a little preparation. Before you even schedule an interview, take a long, hard look at yourself. Be completely honest with yourself. What are you really like and what do you have to offer? For a lot of people, once they hear "completely honest" and "long, hard look," it's the weaknesses that start popping out in neon. "I don't have the kind of experience they're looking for, my computer skills are non-existent, my speaking voice isn't much to speak of . . ." Well, what kind of experience *do* you have? Which of your skills are *not* nonexistent? Which of your personal attributes *are* worth talking about?

As you think about who you are and what you might have to offer an employer, concentrate more and more on the positive and less and less on the negative. At this point, don't even worry about what questions you might get asked. Just build up a repertoire of positive truths about yourself. Scrap "I love to call in sick," in favor of "I'm good at calming people down in a crisis." Try to clear your mind of the puritanical idea that something that's bad about you must automatically be more true than something that's good about you.

Write everything down on a clean sheet of paper. After just a few minutes of thinking about yourself and jotting things down, you should have a good list of positive true things about yourself. The list will probably seem artificial and incomplete to you, maybe even conceited, but remind yourself once more that it's *true*, even though it's not the *whole* truth. True and positive is all we're looking for; comprehensiveness is neither possible nor desirable.

Once you've established a truthful, specific and positive self-image, you need to be similarly honest with yourself about how you fit into the particular position you're applying for. It's a preparation step that a lot of job candidates skip: Take a long, hard look at *the job*. What skills do you think it will require? What kind of person do you think would be a success in this position? To the best of your knowledge, what are the special challenges of this job? What are the benefits of holding this position? How does the person who holds this position benefit the company? How might this job be done better than it's been done in the past? What are the important issues facing the company as a whole?

Remember, knowledge is power. In a later chapter we will provide some quick and easy strategies for finding out more about the company and the position. For now, just list everything you currently know about the job and the company on another sheet of paper.

Now comes the really productive part of this whole exercise: Look at the two lists you've created—the truth about you and the truth about the job—and see where they intersect.

Intersecting Truths

When you get into that interview, you're basically going to have one task to accomplish: You need to show the employer that you are a good match for the position. You do that by taking every opportunity to show the intersection of your truths and the company's needs. It's that simple. And there are always more points of intersection than you expect at first. It's just a matter of looking for them. Which positive aspects of yourself are most important from the point of view of this particular employer?

Maybe in thinking about the challenges faced by the person who holds this position you realized they probably have to deal with a lot of different personalities in the course of the workday. If "flexible" happens to be a true attribute of yours, you've found a potentially powerful point of intersection with the job. Your flexibility is tailor-made to help you deal with all those different personalities!

Now if you're thinking ahead to the actual interview scenario as you read this, you may sense a bit of a flaw in our reasoning, to wit: *"How likely is it that they'll ask me if I would be good at dealing with a lot of personalities?"*

You'd certainly be right that any given question is highly unlikely to be asked. The number of possible questions is just so large that preparing for any specific question is next to pointless. But your objection brings us back to what it really means to be truthful in answering interview questions.

Let's say that one of the questions that actually gets asked in your interview is, "What is your management style?" Many candidates, especially if they're trying very hard to be truthful, freeze up at such a question. Perhaps the most common first thought is, "Um, I don't really have one." How admirably honest! And how unhelpful if spoken aloud.

The first thought that pops into your head is not necessarily as true as it seems. Remember:

- The truth is complex.

- You only get to tell part of it.

- You're the one who decides which part to tell.

If you've done your preparation, when you're asked about your management style you quickly scan the points of intersection between you and the employer and what comes out of your mouth is this: "I've found that, for me, the key to an effective management style is flexibility. In any management situation you deal with a lot of different personalities, and I'm good at making personal connections with lots of different types of people in order to get things done."

Bull's-eye. This answer takes one of your best qualities and shows how you can put it to work for this particular employer, helping to solve a problem that you've already surmised is likely to arise on this job. In the interviewer's head you're probably one step closer to getting the job.

But is that really (truly, honestly) your management style?

Yes. Don't worry about what you're *not* saying. Concentrate on what you *are* saying. What you're saying is something that is true about you and speaks to the interviewer's needs. That's what the interviewer wants you to do. Remember, she's not sitting there with the ideal answer in her head, waiting to see if you'll miraculously land on it. She asked about your management style not as a pop quiz, but to give you an opportunity to offer her something about yourself. So worrying about your answer's incompleteness and imperfection is pointless. The interviewer has a problem—there's a job that won't get done unless she finds somebody to do it—and you're showing her how you can solve that problem for her.

But maybe you think we've still stacked the deck. Haven't we simply chosen another question that's specially designed to fit the hypothesis that you're a flexible person? To a degree, maybe. But we didn't have to. It comes as a surprise to a lot of people that just one intersection between your attributes and the job's requirements is enough to form truthful and effective answers to a wide variety of questions. To prove it, here are some more examples of questions that might not seem to have a lot in common, but for each of them the intersection of "flexible" and "different personalities" would be a great one to offer the interviewer:

"What challenges would you expect to encounter on this job and how would you handle them?"

> *Possible answer*: "It sounds as though I would have to deal with a lot of different people, which means a lot of different personalities. That can be a big challenge. But I'm known for being flexible in my ways of dealing with people, so I'm good at maintaining strong working relationships."

"Are you a leader or a follower?"

> *Possible answer*: "I think I'm someone who feels comfortable taking a leadership position when it's appropriate, but I also enjoy col-

laborating with others. In this job I know I'd be dealing with lots of different personalities in lots of different ways, and I've always been good at being flexible and figuring out when it's best to lead and when it's more constructive to listen and not impose my ideas on other people."

"What appeals to you about this job?"

Possible answer: "I look forward to the opportunity to work with what seems to be a wide variety of personalities. I like looking at problems from various points of view, and I'm flexible enough to develop productive work relationships with many different kinds of people."

Nobody's trying to pretend that the sample answers to these questions are the absolute best possible answers (we do still have other important characteristics of good answers to consider in this book). But you can see how just *one* intersection of personal attributes with company needs can provide effective, truthful answers to a wide range of questions. Of course drawing on the same set of attributes repeatedly over the length of any interview will wear thin, fast. Fortunately, if you do your homework, you'll have *lots* of intersections (more than you may expect) to draw on, and the number of great answers available to you will grow exponentially.

Secret #2:

The Best Answer Is Not Too Short

"Are you a people person?"
"Yes."

"Do you ever have trouble getting along with certain personality types?"
"No."

"Are you looking for a challenge?"
"Most definitely."

"Can you find your own way out?"
"You bet!"

Honesty is obviously not all it takes. If they ask you how well you deal with deadlines and your answer is, "Pretty well, actually"—don't plan on decorating a workstation at this particular address right away. An answer like that falls into the empty answer category. It may be perfectly true, but it tells the interviewer nothing at all about you, except perhaps that you have a modicum of self-esteem. You've given her no reason at all to *believe* your answer, so you've wasted your opportunity. She may try to drag something else out of you by asking you to elaborate, but she's sure to be left with a feeling that you're someone who has to have things dragged out of them. There aren't many jobs for which that's a terrific qualification.

As we've said, the worst way to answer an interview question is to provide only the barest minimum of information. While a "just the facts, ma'am" approach works well in a police-suspect interrogation, most interviewers are looking for something a bit more meaty. But an alarming number of job candidates err on the side of brevity in the interview, perhaps because they're afraid of overstaying their welcome, or they were taught it's not polite to brag, or they grew up in a house where silence was golden and that's just how they are. But the job interview happens to be that very rare opportunity (therapist's couch aside) when someone *wants to make it all about you*. Because all interviews really boil down to this: "Who are you and why should I hire you?"

Put yourself in the interviewer's shoes here for a second. If the person you're interviewing gives short, nonspecific answers, what are you going to think? If you're generous, maybe you'll think it's just that they're a little nervous and you'll try to calm them down and get some substantive answers out of them. But no matter how nice you are, you probably won't be inclined to spend lots of time on that kind of handholding, and you're unlikely to want to hire someone who requires all that work. If you're a less kindly interviewer, you may think this person's terse answers mean they're hiding something, or lying, or cripplingly shy, or not very articulate, or stubbornly defensive, or terrifically boring or . . . Even if you think absurdly positively and decide that this candidate is admirably to the point and does not waste words, at the end of the interview you'll find that that's the sum total of what you have to say about him.

So the big question is: What words should you choose to flesh out an answer? You know you're not supposed to ramble or engage in meaningless small talk. If it really only takes a "Yes" or a "No" to sufficiently answer the question, what can you possibly add that's of value?

Here's a seldom acknowledged and perhaps surprising fact: The interviewer is not necessarily interested in the answer to the question. She's interested in *you*. The questions are just a way to get you talking about some topics that she thinks she might like to hear you talk about.

If she says, "So, do you like living in L.A. so far?" she probably doesn't really care whether you like it or not. She wants to hear you talk about that topic a little bit, as a way of finding out who you are and what you're like. A simple "Yes" is not going to do the trick, even though it answers the question she asked. Maybe what she really means is something more like, "If you like L.A. so far, what is it you like about it, or if you don't, why not?" But that's too long, so she doesn't say all that.

If she asks, "How do you deal with criticism?" she probably cares a little more about the answer to the question, but, "Very well," or, "Not so well," or, "It doesn't make me cry anymore," won't really get to the heart of what she's looking for. (The last option, in particular, may fail to move the interview forward.) Those are all technically responsive to the question, but she's more interested in what you *do* with the question than she is in a straightforward answer.

The real problem with short, simple answers is that they may *tell* the interviewer something, but they don't *show* her anything. And interviewers need to be shown.

The principle is simple. If you *tell* somebody something, they have no reason to believe you. If you want to be persuasive, you need to *show* them why it's true.

Show, Don't Tell

Say your interviewer asks something like, "Do you have experience with Microsoft Word?" Not a brilliant question, or even a very interesting one, but still, please don't say, "Yes," and leave it at that. *Show* her that you know enough about the application to talk intelligently about it. "Oh, yes. At my last job I used a Word template to give the newsletter a new look." Or even: "Yes, I've used it for years and just recently discovered how handy the advanced tab functions are. It seems like there are always more features to learn about." Neither of those responses will get you the job all on its own, but they do take advantage of the opportunity offered by the question. They show you as a person who understands an important tool in a specific way. Suddenly you're somebody who can appreciate details, or cares about efficiency or is always striving to improve—and not just someone who has used a particular word processing program.

If you don't know the program, you can still seize an opportunity: "I haven't used it, because we used WordPerfect at my last job. But I'm a quick study when it comes to software and have taught myself how to use Quicken and Photo Editor (or anything else) on my home computer." Now you've shown the interviewer that you're self-motivated, unintimidated by technology and willing to learn new things. Way to turn lemons into lemonade!

"Show, Don't Tell" should be your motto during your job search. Your résumé has already taken care of the "telling" part. Your presence in the room with this person is your opportunity to show her how those words on the page translate into a real, live human being. And not just *any* real, live human being, but the one who is right for the position that needs to be filled.

Probably the best way to show something about yourself is to do a little telling and then back it up with an example. For example:

Ms. Jones asks, "What's your greatest strength as a salesperson?"

And you respond, "I'd say my people skills are my best asset. I've had customers tell me I'm the only person they'll buy electronics from because I take the time to help them make the choices that best fit their needs without making them feel inferior just because they're not up on the latest equipment."

There's an answer that's not too short. Giving a quick example that shows your people skills in action lifts your answer out of the mundane, robotic and potentially cliché into the realm of the specific, human and engaging.

The Best Answer Is Not Too Long

ONE OF THE MOST ENJOYABLE assignments we ever had was to coach a contestant in a recent Miss USA pageant. She was, not surprisingly, an exceedingly charming and poised young woman. She contacted us for help with her interviewing skills as she prepared for the Miss USA competition. In a way, she was applying for a job—that of Miss USA, goodwill ambassador and national symbol of beauty and prosperity. Not an easy job to get.

Like all beauty contestants, she had plenty of advisors on hair, makeup, dress, walk, diet and smile. She wisely did not come to us for help with those aspects of the competition. She came to us because she felt she needed some special training in the art of answering the questions that would be put to her in private interviews with the judges and perhaps later before an audience of millions, if she advanced into the final rounds of the competition. She had received feedback that the interview was the weakest part of her presentation. She wanted to find out why, and what could be done to fix whatever she was doing wrong.

When we met with her, she did an excellent job with most aspects of the mock interviews we put her through. She was constantly sincere and engaging. She answered with a lot of variety and revealed many wonderful things about her personality and her accomplishments. It was very easy to like her in the interview situation, but it was also clear that she wasn't really nailing it yet. Her answers on the whole were vaguely unsatisfying, even though they contained so much that was good.

Her only problem was that she tended to allow her answers to ramble and trail off. She rarely ended an answer definitively, but instead seemed to talk until she had nothing left to say, or until we, as her interviewers, seemed ready to move on to the next topic. By that point it's too late for any answer to end as strongly as it began.

Our advice to her was simple: *Make a conscious decision to end your answer, even when you may have more to say*. Hopefully, there's always more to say! But saying it all will not necessarily strengthen your answer. Once the interviewer has gotten the idea, repeating it or adding more examples will do little to further impress him.

Gab Is Not Always a Gift

The impulse that leads people to give long-winded answers is usually an admirable one. They are putting themselves out there, showing a willingness to offer whatever information the interviewer might want. They're showing that they're not afraid of social interaction, and that they have opinions they don't mind expressing and experiences they find valuable enough to talk about. These are all good things, and they're the reason it's not good to give an answer that's short and curt, as we discussed in the last section. A certain amount of elaboration is not only valuable, it's vital.

But you can have too much of a good thing. Once you've given an answer and backed it up with an example of what you're talking about, the interviewer will have heard and understood the relevance of what you have to say, and you'll have engaged with her enough to have displayed some personality and social skills. And that's enough. Further examples will rarely add enough value to compensate for making the interviewer impatient.

It's not that the interviewer doesn't have time to listen to one more example or anecdote or clarification, but an answer that goes on too long weakens your presentation in several concrete ways. First, it can make you seem a little desperate, as though you refuse to stop talking until you've covered every possible base and forestalled every possible objection. Talking too much gives the impression that you're working too hard, dancing as fast as you can. It can be exhausting for an interviewer, and doesn't inspire confidence.

Second, the interviewer knows nothing about how you relate to people other than what you demonstrate in your few brief minutes together. Fairly or not, how you act in the interview is frequently seen as a barometer for how you'll act on the job. An overly verbose presentation in the interview—even if well-intended—suggests you might be a chatty Cathy 'round the clock, something few employers want to spend their money on.

Third, an answer that is too long is sure to lose focus along the way. The more detail you pile up, the more opportunities there are for irrelevant tangents, and it takes a superhuman concentration to avoid the temptation to fly off on one of them. Even if you stick pretty close to the point, the more you talk, the more diffuse that point becomes, so that by the end of the answer, the interviewer isn't likely to have a very good sense of what the main idea was. It's therefore harder for him to understand who you are and how you could help him, because the pieces are hard to put together. A jigsaw puzzle with a thousand pieces is just a lot tougher than one with ten.

Luckily, this problem, shared by many a job seeker, is a really easy one to solve. The way to avoid giving an answer that is too long is to *stop talking*.

The only trick is to remember to do it, and to do it consciously. Everybody stops talking eventually, of course, but it really helps to do it before you turn blue. Stopping seems like it should be something that doesn't require any thought, but you give your answer maximum power when you make a conscious decision that what you've said is enough. Then it's time to take a breath, look the interviewer directly in the eye and enjoy seeing where the conversation takes you next.

When our pageant contestant started making a conscious effort to end each answer and trust that it had done its job—which required her to fight the natural tendency to keep elaborating and qualifying what she had just said—her answers improved enormously, and the full power of her terrific personality came through. And the happy ending to the story is that she won! She enjoyed a well-deserved and very successful reign as Miss USA.

Luckily for you, you probably won't need to practice your new skills in front of a national TV audience. The next time you're out with friends or family, make the effort to end your thoughts when they're the strongest. Deleting requests for affirmation—"You know what I mean?"—is a good start. The more you get into the habit of trusting that your communication is clear, the easier it will be to nail your answers when you get to the interview.

The Best Answer Is Uniquely Yours

A COLLEAGUE OF OURS who runs a prestigious acting program for high school students once told us a most instructive interview story. He believed that the best acting students were the ones who were the most interested in learning—not necessarily the ones who had the most acting experience. So, instead of making candidates undergo a traditional audition to determine their acceptance into the program, he sat each one down in an informal interview process where he could get to know who they were, what they were interested in, how they got along with others and so on.

As it turns out, one question he asked proved to be a real make-or-break moment in the interview, in a way no one would have expected. "If you had a Saturday all to yourself, and you could do anything you wanted with anyone you wanted, what would you do?" he asked.

He expected to hear a range of responses, from the mundane (going to the mall, hanging out with friends) to the fantastical (catching dinner with Will Smith, skydiving into Disneyland). What he heard, instead, from the first applicant was, "I would probably read some Shakespeare."

This was surprising but impressive—what an unusual and serious-minded teenager to forgo worldly pleasures in favor of reading something so intellectually demanding! He was primed to offer admission to the student on this basis alone until, later in the day, another candidate gave the very same answer.

As the days went on, he heard this or a similar response from one out of every five or six students. Now, being a longtime teacher and having known lots of teenagers fairly well, he couldn't think of a single one who had actually read Shakespeare just for fun in his or her free time. So this answer now struck him as not only cliché, having been given so many times by so many different students, but also disingenuous. For him, it became a sort of interview poison—every time he heard it, he wanted to dismiss the applicant out of hand. But because he was a fair-minded guy and honestly interested in giving young candidates a chance to get into the program, he usually asked a follow-up question along the lines of, "No, but really . . . what would you do *just for fun*?" To this they generally responded, somewhat sheepishly, that they would go to the mall or hang out with friends or eat dinner with Will Smith.

These students all had one thing in common: their desire to please the interviewer and tell him what they thought he wanted to hear. Unfortunately, what he wanted to hear was something that was unique to each of them and what he got instead was a canned "perfect candidate" answer that made them all seem the same.

Nobody's Perfect (So Stop Trying to Be!)

In determining your success in the job interview, one factor stands out as by far the most important: You. Who you are and what makes you unique.

Now, that sounds awfully simple, but the idea is actually counterintuitive to a lot of people. Most people seem to think success in interviewing consists of molding themselves as closely as possible to a preconceived ideal. Isn't the interview (they hypothetically ask) all about downplaying your personal idiosyncrasies and focusing on the characteristics you share with that elusive but much-sought-after hero, the Perfect Employee?

The key to this apparent paradox is that no one, not even your potential employer, can actually describe to you the Perfect Employee. Real life just isn't that simple. It's as true in the workplace as it is in romance: You could travel halfway around the world in search of your ideal mate, someone incredibly handsome, intelligent and sophisticated, only to return home and find yourself falling in love with the short guy next door with the fabulous sense of humor. Human nature is such that we don't always know what we want until we get it.

If any given employer's Perfect Employee actually exists, you can be sure that person puts his pants on one leg at a time. Wouldn't you agree? He's also as unique and quirky as the next person, guaranteed. That's not to say he doesn't possess traditionally desirable traits. Is he, say, *efficient*? Probably. *Professional*? Probably that, too. But you can be sure he's got his own quirky ways of being efficient and professional, and his employer happens to like the way he does his job. That's what it means to be somebody's Perfect Employee. The qualifications are vague and completely subjective, and the most any employer can truthfully say is that she knows it when she sees it.

So it's completely futile to try to cram yourself into a Perfect Employee mold by making up answers you think the interviewer wants to hear, or to debilitate yourself with the fear that your answers will not be the ones she's looking for. For one thing, you're quite likely to be completely wrong about what she wants to hear. (Some admissions officers might actually *prefer* a teen who admits to spending countless hours on the phone with friends to one who says he holes up reading Shakespeare, even if it were true.) But the more important truth of the matter is that *she herself does not know what she wants to hear*—even if she thinks she does. Everybody in the world is so different from everybody else that it's almost guaranteed that the person who gets the job will do so by impressing the interviewer in a way that the interviewer herself could not have anticipated.

The One and Only . . . You

We coached an excellent candidate for a landscape architecture job who, in spite of his many unique accomplishments, answered most questions in fairly general terms: "I worked on a big historical renovation project that had tight deadlines and we managed to get it done." No matter how much specific prodding we would do, he would always come back to rattling off the names of the building projects on his résumé. We then asked him to tell us about other events and experiences in his life—the ones that weren't relevant to the kind of work he was currently doing. He told us a fascinating story about living and teaching in Haiti during the ouster of Jean Claude "Baby Doc" Duvalier. We were spellbound. Here was a guy who worked under the most adverse conditions imaginable and not only managed to keep his sanity but also was able to modernize the entire curriculum at a school for Haitian teachers before being forced to flee the country amid riots and machine gun fire. What an excellent response to the question of, "How do you handle stressful situations?" or ". . . tight deadlines?" or ". . . working with lots of different people?" . . . or practically anything! Although he resisted mightily at first, complaining that Haiti had nothing to do with the landscape architecture jobs he was interviewing for, we finally convinced him to start working his Haitian experiences into his interview answers once in a while.

He later told us he had come to see that those answers gave him a special way of expressing who he was, what his values were and how he could be expected to perform in a high-pressure situation. And he's been happily employed ever since at one of the area's most prestigious landscape architecture firms.

Getting Beyond Your Résumé

If you've been invited to interview for a job, it's mostly your résumé that has gotten you through the door. The employer was sufficiently impressed by whatever you put on that piece of paper that she decided she should meet you in person.

Now, think for a minute about the résumés of the people who were rejected without an interview. What is it that got them rejected right off the bat? Maybe they didn't have a required degree, or a required minimum amount of applicable job experience. Maybe their résumés had typos or were otherwise unprofessionally presented. Maybe their stated goals were clearly not in line with what the position has to offer.

What that means for you is that everyone who is called in to interview has appropriate degrees and sufficient years of experience, impressively presented résumés, goals that are appropriate to the company and the position and all other general requirements for the job. If Candidate A has more experience than Candidate B, then Candidate B's résumé must show that she has something else going for her (stronger career goals, a better degree) or she wouldn't have made the cut. The differences between the résumés are not enough to determine who should get the job, or the interview wouldn't be necessary at all. So for all intents and purposes, everyone interviewing for the job has *the same résumé*.

It's possible to look at that as bad news. *Uh-oh, everybody who's coming in is qualified!* But you already knew that, didn't you? The point is, if you want to stand out from the crowd, you must use your interview not just to show that you're qualified, but to show exactly *how* you're qualified, in ways that are not reflected in your résumé—ways that make you different from all the other qualified candidates out there.

If Tanya goes into her interview and tries to impress the interviewer with her degree from a prestigious institution, chances are good that she's wasting her time. For one thing, she doesn't know anything about where the other applicants studied, so her degree may not be as impressive as she thinks it is. But the more important point is that the interviewer already knows where she got her degree, because it's on her résumé. If this wonderful degree is somehow enough to get her the job (unlikely), she can relax. But beating the interviewer over the head with a degree he already knows about doesn't separate you from the other candidates in any appreciable way, and it's likely to get annoying. Tanya should assume that she's in the same boat as every other candidate as far as her résumé goes, and seize the interview opportunity by getting *specific*.

What *specifically* is it about this degree that makes her a great candidate for the job in a way that the employer doesn't know about yet? Maybe the department where Tanya studied specializes in hands-on training, or requires a course on the precise skills she'll need in the job she's interviewing for. Now we're talking, because we're getting at how that degree—so generic on paper, no matter how good it sounds—has actually shaped *Tanya* into the uniquely qualified candidate she is.

It's easy to take this example a lot further, though. Tanya is still hanging out in fairly generic territory, because there may well be other applicants who attended the exact same school, or who studied in very similar programs. The point is that it's not so much about the program as it is about how the program has helped make Tanya the person she is. How has she *used* this education?

If Tanya can find an opportunity to explain how she had a mentor in her training program who she developed a great relationship with, who hired her to assist on an important project and gave her some specific insight into real-world work in the field . . . now she's talking about herself more than the education. She's being specific enough that what she's talking about can be helpful to any interviewer, not just one who happens to care about what Tanya guessed he would care about. She's no longer trying to fulfill some preexisting idea of the Perfect Employee with the Perfect Degree. Now she's talking about her *unique* desires and accomplishments. There's no guarantee that any of this is certain to win her the job, of course, but she has successfully seized the opportunity to set herself apart from the competition.

Dare to Be Yourself

A certain amount of bravery is required if you're going to give up on your Perfect Employee impersonation and concentrate on the real you. Jitters are a pretty predictable part of any job interview, of course, so you need bravery just to walk through the door. But people who let their nerves force them into hiding—be it behind generic traits, a defensive front, or half-truths—do themselves a tremendous disservice. The one and only way to really excel at job interviewing is to take the brave leap of showing yourself in all your individuality.

Now, please do remember that this is not a "warts and all" kind of undertaking. We're not talking about the kind of bravery required to let the interviewer in on all your foibles and rashes and indiscretions. There's a special name for that kind of bravery in a job interview. (It's called "idiocy.")

But even talking about your *good* qualities can be a difficult thing to do. The path of least resistance is definitely to tell the interviewer whatever you think she might want to hear and leave out the details of who you really are altogether. For most of us, talking about ourselves in a situation as contrived as an interview is just uncomfortable. Bragging is certainly looked down upon in our society. And when we do get to talking about our good qualities, many of us have an insidious puritanical streak that keeps reminding us that what we're telling is not the whole story, making us feel like liars even when we're telling nothing but the truth. A lot of people say it's best to keep it impersonal, that that's just being professional. But, hey, you *are* a person as well as a professional, and that's something to celebrate, not to hide. More often than not, the kind of person you are—or at least how successfully you convey your personality in the interview—proves the deciding factor in determining who gets the job.

Secret #5

The Best Answer Paints a Picture of Who You Are

THE ANSWER WE'VE BUILT UP so far is one that is truthful, not too short, not too long and uniquely yours. Sounds good.

You've thought a bit about what you have to offer and called to mind some examples to help you back up your claims. You're planning to focus on who you really are and the ways in which you might be able to stand out from the competition. It should be clear by now that this is all about thinking of yourself in the best light and making the interviewer think of you in that way, too.

So, let's get a little more advanced. It's time to make sure that you're presenting yourself not only clearly and positively, but also *vividly*. You want all those great traits and illustrative examples to come shining through, so the interviewer gets a strong, lasting picture of you and your unique qualifications without having to work too hard.

One of your best tools for doing all of this is a good little story about yourself, something a little more developed than the quick examples we've been talking about up until now. A story is not a ramble, of course, and because it takes up a bit of time you have to make sure its value and relevance are especially clear. But a well-told story, with a strong point, is a great way to make the interviewer's understanding of you even more vivid and enduring. It paints a picture of who you are, leaving no doubt in the interviewer's mind about what your potential assets are. They'll be there in Technicolor, impossible to miss.

As with everything else, preparation is the key. You'll want to come to the interview armed with a couple of stories that might help bolster an answer, and you'll plan to be on the lookout for a valid opportunity to tell one of them.

Stories That Matter

So what makes for a good story to tell in an interview?

Well, a blow-by-blow account of the traffic that made you late to the interview would be an example of a really bad story to tell. Yet many an interviewee seems to think that kind of thing is worth doing for some reason. It may seem like a good way to establish a personal connection, but there are at least two good reasons not to tell the traffic story: 1) It does not make you look good, and 2) It is not interesting.

To be worthy of telling in an interview, a story should center around an experience that will help the interviewer see why you would be a good person to hire in this position. Don't tell any stories that don't do that. You may notice a picture of a cat on the interviewer's desk and be tempted to launch spontaneously into that cute story about your adorable Fluffy and the golden retriever next door—thinking you're establishing rapport, or something—but because the topic is so trivial, you're most likely to come off as unprofessional, and you're actually just wasting time.

It's important to share your personality and uniqueness in the interview, yes, but you have to do it in ways that are relevant to your candidacy for the position. Mention that you have a cat, if you like, but you can pretty much leave it at that. Pets and traffic are not good interview story material. They tell the employer nothing about you at your professional best, and your kitten and your gridlock are never as interesting to other people as they are to you. If you prepare a couple of stories that will show you at your professional best, you won't be prone to this kind of random chatter, which can be brutal when you're nervous.

So a story has to show something helpful about you and it has to be interesting. That's not to say it has to make you look like the Messiah and be the Most Interesting Story Ever Told. How about some professional achievement you're proud of? It doesn't have to be huge. A time when you were able to help someone out of a tough spot? The circumstances that led to your last promotion? That clever remark you made that eased tension at the big meeting?

All we're really talking about is a slightly more developed version of an example that you might use to back up a claim. You say you're a good motivator? We need an example before we're going to believe you. And maybe you can really prove it to us with the right anecdote. Nothing too long and involved, but something with enough detail that it's easy to *picture* your motivational skills in action and see how they could benefit the particular workplace you're applying to.

So, a good story illustrates one or more of your good qualities, seems likely to be interesting to the employer and is pretty short, but detailed. The details are what lift a story out of boring résumé-land into the world of the lively interview. This is your chance to be really specific. Give us a time when you motivated your colleagues to exceed their previous performance, and give it to us *vividly*. Exactly what results did you pull out of your fellow workers, and how exactly did you make that happen? In other words, what unusual things did you do or say and what were the specific responses you received? Don't be afraid to think in dramatic terms: Most good interview stories have well-drawn characters, specific action, meaningful dialogue, a splash of conflict (or obstacles that have to be overcome) and, ultimately, a happy ending.

An example: We worked with a guy named Jeremy who had facilitated all the various activities that took place in a university theater building. He was a great interviewee, and his secret weapon was his story about how he won the support of a bitterly infighting faculty with competing needs for the space. He quickly sketched the personalities of the two main characters (a hotheaded drama teacher and a stubborn history lecturer who liked to give the silent treatment) and then related how he scheduled a meeting with the two of them and dared to propose—in the most polite and well-meaning terms, of course—some ways in which they could significantly improve the life of the campus by making a few concessions: If one would agree to hold lectures an hour later two days a week, the other could make sure that all rehearsal props were removed from the stage area before those lectures began. Jeremy even offered to enlist the help of student volunteers in keeping the space tidy. He showed his "people skills" in action by describing how these two foes softened as a result of his efforts. They didn't like each other any better at the end of the meeting, but they had both become Jeremy's allies. It was a great story—good characters, plenty of human interest, and it told a lot about certain traits that could make Jeremy a great asset to an employer.

Another great feature of that story of Jeremy's is its flexibility. It's specific without being limited in its applicability. It says something somehow central to who Jeremy is, so it could be used in response to a wide variety of questions. What are you like to work with? Tell us about an achievement you're proud of. How do you handle conflict in the workplace? Do you feel comfortable taking initiative? How would you describe your communication skills? What special skills would you bring to this position? What's your greatest strength? And when you think about it, the likelihood that one of these questions—or some variation—will actually come up is extremely high. A slam-dunk for Jeremy.

It's worth mentioning, by the way, that Jeremy clearly had not *memorized* this story, as in knowing it word for word. He had prepared it enough that he knew the point and which details he wanted to include, and knew he could keep it focused and not get rambly. So he told it with a feeling of knowing what he was talking about, but it remained spontaneous. There's no such thing as too much preparation for an interview, but there is definitely such a thing as the wrong *kind* of preparation. Memorizing is almost always the wrong kind, because when you've planned every word that's going to come out of your mouth, it's hard not to sound "canned." The interview is your opportunity to be the real, live you. A stilted delivery will certainly get in the way of that. So don't let your preparation become a chore.

To help get you thinking about some widely applicable stories you yourself might have to tell, see where the following prompts take you. (If you think you've never experienced any of these situations, you're just wrong.)

Think of a time when you:

- went beyond the call of duty

- surprised people with an unexpected solution to a problem

- earned a special commendation

- turned an opponent into an ally

- lightened someone else's load

- discovered that you'd become the one people turn to

- saved your company some money

- improved the efficiency of a system

- overcame a seemingly insurmountable obstacle

After you've chosen a story you might tell, think about it in greater detail.

Remind yourself:

- how the situation started out

- how it was different after you took action

- exactly what that action was

- how the accomplishment made you feel

- how the accomplishment benefitted someone else

- what that person said about the job you did

- what it is about you that made the accomplishment possible

Experiment with these details a little bit and you'll find you've got yourself some interesting and vivid stories that show you at your best and are flexible enough to use as part of your answer to a wide variety of questions. If you want to practice, try working one into a chat with a colleague or a dinner conversation with a friend. And make sure you have fun sharing the details. The more you enjoy telling a story, the more someone else will enjoy hearing it.

The Best Answer Demonstrates Knowledge of the Company

LET'S SAY YOU'RE INTERVIEWING for a store manager position with one of the country's fastest-growing purveyors of the four-dollar cup of coffee commonly known as the latte. You're an excellent match for the job, having spent the last two years doubling the profits of a store owned by the company's biggest competitor. (In fact, you were so successful that your last employer could hardly bear to see you go, but hey . . . your spouse got a big promotion, which meant moving to another city and what were you going to do?) So here you are, an outstanding candidate for the job at hand. You've spent some time thinking about where your strengths intersect with the needs of the position and you're prepared with specific examples of the ways you've increased revenue, motivated employees, improved customer service and excelled in just about every way imaginable as a barista beyond compare.

You walk into the interviewer's office feeling appropriately confident. After a bit of pleasant chitchat (it turns out he's from your hometown!), he lobs a softball at you: "How has your past experience prepared you for this job?"

Yeah, baby. This one's going out of the ballpark!

"I'm used to working in a fast-paced environment. As a senior manager with Java Junkies I was responsible for the fastest growing store in downtown Cleveland. I believe I can use my management experience with alternative marketing and product promotion to rapidly expand your customer base, bringing in a far younger crowd in addition to the coffee regulars."

Good answer, right? Succinct, includes important information about past accomplishments, even sets an agenda for your future with the company. Your interviewer will surely ask you to elaborate, which will lead you to the spectacular story you've prepared about the all-night "Pajava Party" you and your employees introduced, filling the store with hip, coffee-loving teens on the first Saturday night of every month.

Except that's not what happens. "Oh . . . we're not interested in packing our stores to the gills or getting young people hooked on coffee," the interviewer replies.

A swing and a miss! A strong, confident swing, yes, but a miss nonetheless because it failed to take into account this company's particular pitch. You see, if you had done a little research on the company you would have realized that they're *the other guys* in the latte business— dedicated to providing a relaxed and comfortable environment for sophisticated coffee drinkers. Had you known that, you could have led with a story about how you improved barista response time, or instituted a sampling policy for exotic blends or increased customer satisfaction scores by 17 percent—all of which were just as true as the example you gave, but likely to be much more appealing to *this particular employer* than the prospect of a bunch of buzzed teenagers overcrowding the store.

• • •

It's possible (in fact, common) for a job candidate to leave an interview having made a great impression as an experienced professional with brains to spare, a great attitude and a terrific personality—and to find out the next day that he didn't get the job. Sure, sometimes it's because the boss's nephew got it, but more often it's because this great candidate didn't make the case that he was the right match for *this job at this company at this time.* The crucial step that so many otherwise excellent interviewees leave out is to help the interviewer connect the dots by demonstrating an accurate and enthusiastic understanding of the company and the position.

Often the best way to stand out in a job interview is to show the employer just how well you'll fit in. And that takes some research.

Getting to Know Them

In the age of the Internet, it's never been easier to arm yourself with exactly the information you need. Make friends with company websites. This is where you'll discover how employers define themselves—what they do, what their values are and how they are using their employees to achieve their goals. If you're lucky, you might also find company newsletters posted that give you specific information about current activities. Jot down notes about things that interest you or areas in which you feel you could make a unique contribution.

If the company is a major one, you can also go to your favorite Internet search engine and check for recent news stories, or even type in the interviewer's name to see if she's quoted anywhere. All of this should help you get a better sense of what you each have to offer the other.

If the company doesn't have a website, or if you simply want to delve deeper, you can always call the front office and request a brochure, annual report or any other materials they typically send to prospective clients, investors or the general public.

Often, the best sources of information about a company are the informal ones—people working in that organization or in similar organizations who can give you an insider's view of what goes on in the business. If you can think of somebody who might have some knowledge to pass on, give them a call.

If your research isn't turning up anything worthwhile, go to your local library (or better yet, a university library) and check with the reference librarian. He can guide you to comprehensive listings of nonprofits, law firms, Fortune 500 companies and much more.

Once you feel you've got a picture of what the company does, how they do it and what the future might hold for them, you can put your pencil down. You don't need to learn everything—just enough to help you speak intelligently about why you are a good match for the company and the job.

Here are some questions to think about as your interview approaches. If you can't answer all of them, that's okay (remember: the interview is not a test). Use what you know to shape your responses to the interviewer's questions. Use what you don't to guide the conversation when the interviewer inevitably asks, "Do you have any questions for me?"

- What's the primary purpose of the company (what do they do)?

- What is the prevailing philosophy of the company (why and how do they do what they do)?

- Who do they serve?

- Who are their competitors and how are they similar or different?

- What is the basic organizational structure of the company?

- How does the position for which you are applying fit into this structure?

- To the best of your knowledge, what are the primary responsibilities of the position?

- What salary range could you expect for this position?

- What about the position or company most appeals to you?

- How formal or informal is the atmosphere?

- What would you describe as the major strengths of this company?

- In your opinion, what are the major needs of this company?

So now you have some knowledge about the company. How can you demonstrate it in an interview in a way that will bring you closer to receiving a job offer?

Well, once again let's start with what not to do: No one is interested in hearing an interviewee spew facts about the company or spout statistics from the website unless these serve the larger purpose of showing how you are a good match for the company. So, "I was excited to learn that your widgets have earned a top 15 percent rating in consumer quality surveys for the past ten years," is a waste of breath unless you add something like: ". . . because quality assessment and customer retention are two of the areas that I was most focused on in my last job."

Stay on your toes and be on the lookout for opportunities to make connections. Follow the lead of these excellent candidates:

Tamara (ceramic engineer applying to a large manufacturing company): "Well, one of the things I'd like to be doing in five years is making significant contributions in your research department. Your recent citation as one of the top ceramic research firms in the country was one of the main things that attracted me to this position."

Bob (applying to be an administrative assistant at a small nonprofit): "I think the greatest skill I can bring to this position may well be my ability to coordinate lots of logistical details, as I did when I was the facilities manager at Belwood Charter School. I noticed on your website that you're moving to a big new space, which is exciting, and I think I could help with many aspects of the move."

Reginald (applying to be a marketing consultant at an indie record label): "I know teenagers are a big part of your target market, and one challenge I would expect to face would be figuring out what they're going to want to listen to next year. But in addition to my experience with various trend analysis tools, I happen to have three teenagers of my own, so I feel pretty tuned in to what they're listening to. As tuned in as an old fogey can be, anyway."

As you already know, your most important task is to help the interviewer see how your skills and experiences (also known as your "truths") intersect with their needs. A little research is your best tool for discovering those intersections.

Proper research will also enable you to ask insightful questions of your interviewer and to honestly determine whether you and the company have a lot to offer each other. It will enable you to impress the interviewer as someone who would not take long to be brought "up to speed" with how the company functions. Most important, it will enable you to tell the prospective employer why you want the job in a way that will be specific and meaningful. No matter what else happens in the interview, you must find at least one opportunity to express a genuine interest in the job, and the reasons you give must be based on accurate knowledge of the position and the company.

A final caveat: As you explore ways of incorporating your understanding of the company into your interview presentation, please remember the old adage about a little knowledge being a dangerous thing. Walking into an interview and proclaiming, "I noticed that your website is outdated," is rarely a winning strategy, even if web design is one of the greatest skills you could bring to a company. Maybe the interviewer himself designed that site, or is especially proud of it or, even if he isn't, doesn't want some smug "outsider" offering up unasked-for criticisms. Instead, you might observe how the company is using the website as an important tool in its business promotion and express your interest in working on web-related issues.

Keep it positive, keep it relevant and you'll keep helping the employer see you as the right person for the job and the company.

Here's a list of information sources you might find helpful:

- Company website

- Company or organization brochures, newsletters, annual reports

- Newspaper, magazine or Internet articles

- Internet sites devoted to business listings (e.g., Vault.com, Hoover's Online, and salary.com)

- Former or current employees

- The sales or PR department of the company

- Company receptionists

- Reference librarians

- Industry specialists and competing companies

- Company suppliers

- Business Registries (e.g., *Standard and Poor's Register of Corporations, Directors and Executives, Dunn and Bradstreet's Million Dollar Directory, Ward's Business Directory of U.S. Public and Private Companies, The New Nonprofit Almanac and Desk Reference*)

- Local Chambers of Commerce, Better Business Bureau, trade associations

Secret #7:

The Best Answer Addresses the Question Behind the Question

MEET PETER, PAUL AND MARY. They're in need of jobs. They're doing interviews. Please learn from their mistakes.

Here, for your analysis, are their answers to the question, "How do you deal with stress?"

Peter said, "Usually if a day has been really stressful, I go home and take a hot bath. That always helps me relax for the evening."

Paul said, "Actually, stress is never a problem for me. I'm a pretty laid-back kind of guy."

Mary said, "Oh. I get it. You're wondering why I'm so stressed-out at the moment, aren't you? Well, I'm not usually like this, I swear, but traffic on the way here was insane. You would not believe what this guy in a Pathfinder did to me. . . ."

We firmly believe that there's no such thing as a single answer that's bad enough to sink an interview, but this trio could have taken much better advantage of the opportunity this question offers them.

Peter may be charmingly open about his personal habits, but he has pretty clearly crossed into Too Much Information territory. Not that there's really such a thing as too much information, but there's definitely such a thing as too much of the *wrong kind of information*. And volunteering details about your evening ablutions is unlikely to help the interviewer understand anything about how you'll be behaving during the day, which she probably cares a lot more about.

Paul would seem to be doing the Perfect Employee thing, pretending to be the stressless clone he thinks employers are looking for. He must also think employers are extremely stupid. He experiences stress whether he knows it or not, so he's presenting himself as either ludicrously lacking in self-awareness, or a liar. Neither one scores him a lot of points.

And Mary. Poor insecure Mary. She jumped to a silly conclusion about the interviewer's motives for asking the question, and it led her down the path of desperate self-justification and boring traffic stories.

These answers go astray in three very different ways, giving uniquely poor impressions of each interviewee, but they have one very important thing in common. Their weaknesses all arise from the same root cause: an unhelpful interpretation of the question that was asked.

"Why Do You Ask?"

The question "How do you deal with stress?" might seem like a fairly straightforward one, but all interview questions require at least a little interpretation. The step that Peter, Paul and Mary failed to take was to think productively about the interviewer's point of view.

Peter—he of the evening baths—apparently did not think about the interviewer's point of view at all. He does not seem to have considered why the interviewer asked the question. He just gave the answer that popped into his head. He seems to have been truthful and sincere, just not very good at giving the interviewer a reason to hire him.

Paul's denial—his claim that he never experiences stress—seems to come from a common misinterpretation of the interviewer's agenda. He seems to be one of those job candidates who thinks the point of the questions is to see how many he can get right. In a perfect world, what would be best for the employer? For her employees never to experience stress. Therefore, a question about dealing with stress must be a trick question. Give the *right* answer: No stress here, no ma'am.

Of course, for the reasons given above, that's not going to work. The "right" answer almost always smacks of sucking up. But, more important for the issue at hand, it arises from a really *unhelpful interpretation* of what the interviewer is up to. Paul has posited an adversarial relationship, like that between a cringing pupil and a teacher with a ruler. And he dutifully plays the role of the straight-A student, giving the answer that a lot of books would tell him is foolproof.

But the problem is that this way of looking at the interview scenario is just plain incorrect. Anyone who has ever actually interviewed someone for a job will tell you that they're interested in finding out who the interviewee is, what he's like and what his qualifications seem to be. That involves listening carefully to each interviewee's answers and trying (completely subjectively) to decide how well he will fulfill this particular position in the particular culture of this particular company. That's a much more subtle and complicated task than any set of right-or-wrong questions could ever accomplish. Yes, there may be a few interviewers out there who go into the interview with that kind of rigid, pop-quiz mentality, but they're likely to be dictatorial weirdos whose predetermined answers are so idiosyncratic to their own way of seeing the world that you stand a one-in-a-billion chance of landing on their "correct" answer, so why try? And, by the way, who really wants to work for that person, anyway?

When he says he never experiences stress, Paul may actually think he's just being himself, presenting himself as the devil-may-care, easy-going chum he likes to think of himself as. Even if we assume that he's being completely straightforward and sincere, not trying at all, even subconsciously, to impress the interviewer with the right answer, there's still a big problem here. The question clearly presupposes that there will be stress involved with this job. The interviewer is in some way expressing a concern, and an unsubstantiated claim that her concern is invalid is unlikely to win her over.

So Paul's Perfect Employee syndrome leads to a misinterpretation of the interviewer's motivations in asking the question, and Peter's "straightforward and sincere" approach fails to take the interviewer's motivations into account at all. To take full advantage of an interview question, you must do your best to address *the question behind the question.*

Please understand that we are not trying to say that your interviewer is trying to trick you in any way, refusing to ask about what she really wants to know. She *is* asking what she really wants to know. What you have to do is think just a little bit about why she wants to know it.

We are also not saying (as many other interview books *do* say) that each question represents one and only one "question behind the question" and you better get it right or forget about it. We don't claim to be able to identify the question behind every question, because each interviewer is different, each interviewee is different, each job is different, etc.

What we *are* saying is that you must not overlook the fact that the interviewer has certain needs in the interview, and she asks the questions as a way of trying to satisfy those needs. If you tell her about the baths you like to take, you may be satisfying some odd need of your own, but you're clearly not satisfying hers. If you suggest that her question in some way doesn't apply to you, she's unlikely to believe you, so no one's needs are being met.

Of course, you could make the worst mistake of all and do what

Mary did. Mary definitely tried to take the interviewer's needs into account, and took a stab at the possible question behind the question. Unfortunately, Mary seems to have decided that the question behind the question was, "Are you going to be a big problem for me, you stressed-out freak?"

It's a sad fact that when we human beings get to speculating about each other's motives, we tend to become somewhat suspicious and mistrustful. "What did she mean by that?" usually translates as, "She must have meant something malicious by that!" Mary's assumption seems to be that the interviewer is out to trip her up in some way, to uncover all her weaknesses and failings. To consider the interviewer's reasons for asking a question is therefore to get defensive.

Absurd as Mary's interpretation may seem to those of us who are not, right at this very second, undergoing a job interview, it's important to remember that when you're the one sitting across from that potential employer, you may not be thinking as clearly as you are now. The stakes may suddenly seem very high, and it's possible that your instinctive fight-or-flight behaviors may start to take over to a certain extent. That's the value of reading this book. You're preparing the right mindset before walking into the room. You are armed against the power of Mary's negative kind of thinking, because you're prepared to recognize it as hogwash the second your subconscious starts throwing it at you.

So, while Peter, Paul and Mary may be leaving on the next jet plane, you will hopefully be here to stay. And the power of positive thinking has a lot to do with that.

Consciously choose to interpret the interviewer's question in a helpful way. Since you cannot know definitively what the question behind the question is, give it your best shot. Assume the interviewer asked the question in order to satisfy a need, and then do your best to help satisfy that need in a way that will show her that you're the person she's looking for.

Optimal Interpretation

So what might be a better approach to "How do you deal with stress?" Rather than avoiding the issue or interpreting the question in a way that is defensive or counterproductive, think for a second or two about what need might lie behind this question. A strong choice would be to assume that the interviewer expects stress to be a part of the job for a normal person and wants to make sure you have some way of getting the job done even when it gets stressful. So perhaps the question behind the question is: "Can you demonstrate to me that you will be successful working in a high-pressure environment?"

What's a truthful answer for you? Do you take a sixty-second time-out at your desk, after which you're ready to take on all stress-inducers? Are you especially good at talking out conflicts so that they don't get out of hand? Can you give an example of a stressful situation in a past job and how you handled it in a productive way?

These answers, while maybe not exactly what the interviewer thought she was fishing for, present a strong image of you as a competent employee. For that reason, they will probably get you one step closer to the ultimate Yes. And let's face it: You can't read the interviewer's mind. There are any number of reasons why she might have asked a particular question, so pick one that works well for you. If it turns out she needs different information from what you gave her, trust that she'll ask another question.

Here's another one to ponder. Say the interviewer says simply, "Tell me about yourself." It's not hard to feel threatened by even such a banal request as that. It's so vague. But if, *"What's she up to now?"* and, *"Can she tell I hate my mother?"* are the first things that run through your head, try to get a grip. First of all, you should already have asked yourself, *What's the* opportunity *here?* And with this particular request, it's wide open. She has invited you to tell her pretty much any- thing you want! Now *that's* an opportunity!

Why might she have asked that question? There are plenty of un- helpful possibilities to choose from, of course: She asked it because somebody told her about your unfortunate run-in with the mayor. She asked it because she's an idiot who couldn't come up with an original question if her life depended on it. She asked it because she's trying to pick you up.

But *maybe* she asked it because she's intentionally trying to give you an opportunity to say whatever you want to say, without the con- straints of a more specific question. Maybe she's trying to take some of the pressure off, rather than put more on. Maybe she simply wants to hear anything you have to say about the relevant experiences that have brought you to this moment in your life when you would want to work for her. Well, that shouldn't be so hard.

Need a few more examples of how this all works in the real world? Look no further:

5 Common Questions and the Questions Behind Them

What They Ask:	What They Might Want to Know:
1. Why did you leave your last position?	Are you reliable?
	Are you easy to work with?
	Will you stay in this job for a significant period of time?
2. Why do you want this job?	Are your expectations in keeping with the realities of the position?
	How long will you stay?

What They Ask:	What They Might Want to Know:
	What unique contributions do you see yourself making?
3. Are you a fast learner?	Will you need a lot of supervision?
	Are you willing to take risks and try new things?
	Will you go above and beyond the basic responsibilities of the position?
4. What's your greatest weakness?	Are you honest about yourself?
	How do you handle a potentially stressful question?
	Do you have any traits that might weaken your performance in this position?
5. What salary are you looking for?	Are your goals compatible with what we have to offer?
	How much do you know about our company and the position?
	Why do you want this job?

Now, keep in mind, these are only *possible* questions behind the question. There are countless others, and part of your job in the interview is to simply *decide* on a strong and positive reason why the question was asked. As we've said before, the interviewer wants nothing more than for you to be the one (then she can end the whole interview process and get back to doing her real work!) so the reason she's asking you *any* question is to get closer to an answer to her ultimate question: "Why should I hire you?"

So let's look specifically at how addressing a question behind the question can bring you both closer to the answer you want. Take the first example on our list: "Why did you leave your last position?" Let's imagine the increasingly common scenario (and maybe even the reason you're holding this book in your hand) that you're looking for work because you were laid off when your company went through a process of restructuring.

Well, if you simply look at the question itself, it seems she wants to know why you are no longer working at your prior job. An appropriate response to that question might be, *"I was laid off when my company went through a process of restructuring and my department was downsized."* Okay, you've satisfied perhaps one basic need—she knows you weren't fired for being an ax murderer—but you haven't really moved the conversation forward by addressing her higher-level needs. Your answer was good defense, at best.

So now, instead of just taking the question at face value, let's look at how you can use the opportunity to positively address some potential underlying questions. *"When my company went through a process of restructuring, my department was downsized and I was laid off. In some ways, I look at it as a positive thing because, even though I had terrific co-workers and really liked the company atmosphere* (translation: I get along with people), *there weren't many opportunities to grow in the position and I'm looking for a place to begin a long-term career* (translation: I'd like to be here for a while)."

Now you're talking. You've used a potentially nerve-wracking question *(Oh no, she wants me to admit I lost my last job!)* to provide some useful information you were hoping to give anyway and you've answered a couple of unspoken questions along the way. Now, if she wants, the interviewer can follow up on a few of the themes you've offered up. *(How were you hoping to grow in your last position? What did you like about the atmosphere of your former company? What constitutes long-term for you?)* And every follow-up represents a new opportunity to move the relationship forward.

The biggest favor you could do for yourself is to get into the habit of thinking about each question from the point of view of a benevolent employer who has a problem (she needs an employee) and hopes that you'll provide the solution (you'll be the employee). Once you've done that, it's easy to see how each question behind the question is another chance for you to speak directly to her needs and demonstrate your worth.

The Best Answer Is Active

ARE YOU A PERSON who sits around waiting to be told what to do? Do you like to be a pawn in someone else's game? Is "puppet" a good word for the role you most like to play?

If so, don't spread it around. If you're that passive, there's probably a machine that can do any job better than you can, and machines are usually cheaper labor. They'll beat you out for the job every time.

Most of us don't think of ourselves as habitually passive and spineless, yet an awful lot of people allow themselves to come across that way in a job interview. For some reason, the strange power dynamic—created mostly in the interviewee's head—can wipe out all possibility of taking initiative of any kind.

It's the darnedest thing. Why would otherwise vivacious people retreat into submissiveness in an interview setting? At the risk of overstating the obvious, look no further than the fear factor. Fear of failure, fear of making fools of ourselves, fear of giving the wrong answer, fear of the unknown, fear of the known, fear of fear, and the list goes on.

And fear almost always translates into avoidance. We strive to avoid saying anything foolish, wrong or whatever else, and consequently put our focus in the worst possible place—on what we're *not* doing rather than what we *are* doing. In order to survive the experience, we set the interview bar too low: *My job is just to answer her questions and not mess up.*

But you've got to remember that the job is not yours to lose—it's yours to *win*. And, as every good sportsperson knows, you can't do that by playing it safe and protecting some mythical lead.

When the interviewer asks you a question, she doesn't want you to try to please her any more than you would want a friend or a mate to constantly sublimate their true thoughts and feelings until they saw which way the wind was blowing. When the interviewer asks you a question, she wants you to *advance the conversation*. To put something interesting out there that will help you both understand and appreciate each other better. Too passive a stance will make you seem like a person who would be unable to be proactive on the job, and that's probably not the kind of person she wants to hire.

We're not saying storm into the office and start off by demanding the best view and an exorbitant salary. Politeness and deference to the interviewer are a must. The power dynamic is not entirely fictional; she really is the boss, and inappropriate usurping of her authority will get you nothing but shown to the door. You are not the main person controlling the interview.

But if you take no control at all, you risk 1) being seen as a weakling, 2) missing opportunities to sell yourself and 3) leaving the interview without having learned as much as possible about how good a match you and this job really are.

Being active in the interview means *doing things* other than simply responding to questions. Not random things. Handstands and Jimmy Stewart impersonations rarely help.

Engaging the interviewer in a good conversation might be a good idea, though. *Thinking* about her questions, your answers and your developing relationship might be a good idea, too. As would *assessing* how the interview is going. *Asking* some questions of your own, *interpreting* the interviewer's words and *promoting* what's uniquely positive about you—all of these would be good things to be doing along the way.

The italicization in the last paragraph is there to emphasize that it's all about the verbs. They're the *doing* part. Once again, we're talking about an area that résumés are usually deficient in. No matter how active you try to make your résumé, even if you type a lot of verbs into it (*achieved* this, *increased* that), as a static piece of paper there's not much that it can really *do*. Résumés are about what's already done. The interview is your chance to do some more, to show yourself in action.

So you want to come into the interview armed with a few verbs— performable actions—that will give you some options for what to do other than sit there and fulfill the most basic requirement of getting the questions answered. Here are a few productive ones to focus on.

ENGAGE

The best interviews are enjoyable conversations: both parties comfortable, learning interesting things about each other, each appreciating the best of the other's personality.

Everybody can probably agree that it's not a good interview if nobody enjoys it. But some of the very worst interviews may be conversations that are actually quite enjoyable, but only to the interviewee. He's off and running, having a grand old time, but boring or annoying the interviewer to death. Lots of fun for him, until a few weeks go by with no job offer in sight and the wolves start baying at the door.

Much of this book has focused on how you can satisfy the interviewer's needs during the interview. Her need to enjoy the interview is not at the top of that list—more important, certainly, are her needs to fill the position with the best candidate and to understand as much as possible about what kind of employee you would be—so the enjoyment factor is easy to overlook. She doesn't have to have the time of her life— you're definitely not there to *entertain* her, and it would probably be disastrous to try—but if you're able to *engage* her to a certain degree, you'll raise yourself above the level of the average candidate who's concentrating only on the basics.

So what does it mean to engage somebody? Engage them in what? Well, in this case, it's not a debate or an arm wrestling match, but simply an interesting conversation of some kind. That may sound like a tall order in the interview situation, until you realize how instinctively you do just that in other scenarios.

The important thing to recognize is that you only do it when you want to. Like when you're single and lonely and you encounter an appealing person. Under the right circumstances, you will engage this person in conversation. If the desire to do so is there, you will do it.

The only difficulty in the job interview situation is that the desire is not usually there. So you just have to remember to want it: Go into the interview with the idea that engaging in a productive, pleasant conversation would be a great thing. And then you'll do it, and probably in the same way you would do it in a potentially romantic situation: by *focusing on the other person.*

The interviewer is a person, too. Keeping that in mind is the first step toward establishing a meaningful relationship. Remind yourself to care about what she thinks. Remember to listen actively, so that you stand a chance of *figuring out* what she thinks. Say things that will show that you're interested in what she thinks. One of the best ways to do that is to ask questions.

Asking an intelligent question or two shows that you're curious, that you're prepared, that you understand enough about the company and the position to want to go deeper, that you care about details and that you're not cowed into submission by the interview process. But the best part is that questions require answers, and hence automatically engage the interviewer.

We've already warned about trying to engage the interviewer about her cat or the evils of traffic—too much about the weather or her health are bad ideas, as well—but questions about the job, the company, even the interviewer's specific roles, can keep the conversation productive and appropriate while increasing the give-and-take and adding variety and liveliness to the proceedings. An enjoyable conversation might even result!

THINK

Agreed. You should do some thinking in the interview. Lack of thinking is the ultimate passivity.

What kind of thinking should you do? A lot of cerebral activity centered around the size of the interviewer's nose (or your own) will get you nowhere. Continuous analysis of your embarrassing social skills will prove equally unproductive.

We've already covered lots of types of thinking that you should be doing during the interview, but we take this opportunity to urge you to remember to do it, to do it appropriately and to do it productively. And to value thinking as an integral part of the interview.

It's okay to take *time* to think. If you really believe that thinking is an integral and valuable part of the interview, it follows that it's okay to devote some time to it. Yet one effect of stress is that it can make you open your mouth before you've adequately decided what should come out of it. Trust that the interviewer also values thinking. Taking a moment to consider the question and breathing before answering will serve you well.

But thinking goes on continuously, of course. You should be thinking throughout the interview, not just when it comes time to formulate an answer. So that moment before you start speaking should be brief. No matter how much internal brain activity is going on, it's hard to appear active when all the interviewer can see is a long stretch of sitting and breathing. A couple seconds of thinking should be enough to get you confidently launched into your answer, then the bulk of the brain power comes into play while you're actually doing the talking.

And what those brain waves should be doing is searching your memory banks for relevant traits, examples or stories to include in your answer; remembering not to let your answer be too short or too long; focusing on what is true and unique to who you are; painting a vivid picture of you and your qualifications; and positively interpreting the question behind the question. If all that isn't enough to keep you busy and active, nothing is.

ASSESS

Another very important action to keep in your arsenal is the verb *assess*. Assessing is a specific subcategory of *thinking*, of course, but in the sense we mean it here it's a new, more holistic kind of thinking than we've discussed so far.

We're talking about actively assessing how the interview is going. Not in the sense of whether or not you're blowing it, but in the sense of how well you've taken advantage of your opportunities along the way, so you can decide which of your interviewing tools would serve you best in the remainder of the interview.

Has the interviewer been responding especially enthusiastically to examples of your conflict-resolution skills? If so, it might be a good idea to work in a story about that. Are the stories you thought would work so well seeming to have little positive effect on her? Maybe it would be best not to tell any more. Actively assessing which techniques are getting the best response will tell you which ones to keep going with and which ones to drop.

You should also assess your own performance by considering how well you're "mixing it up." This book presents a lot of options, and using them all at various times throughout the interview will ensure the best performance. In other words, if you've been forgetting to tell stories, it may be time to try one. Do you notice that your answers are all tending to be rather short, or all rather long? Mix it up. Find a way to mention a great trait of yours that hasn't come up yet. Ask a question. Work in some knowledge about the company and the position that shows you know what you're talking about.

In addition to assessing your use of techniques and their apparent effect on the interviewer, you should be using the interview as your chance to assess the company and the position for yourself. Does this person seem like someone you would like to work for? Is the position more or less interesting to you now than it was before the interview started? How is what you're learning about the place—through what the interviewer tells you directly and through whatever other clues come to you from her expressions and the environment and the other people you encounter—affecting your sense of both what you could get out of working here and what you have to offer? You're probably looking into the possibility of other positions elsewhere as well, so you should be assessing what might make you choose this job over another one in case you get more than one offer.

PROMOTE

Unfortunately, this action is something of a lost art and too frequently confused with slick self-aggrandizement. But trace "promote" back to its Latin roots and you'll find it means "to move forward," which is exactly what you want to do with the interview conversation. You want to move it to the next place, the place that helps the interviewer see you no longer as a job applicant, but as a colleague. So how do you do that?

You do it by promoting a positive image of who you are. From the way you nod during a question, to the enthusiasm you project about the company, to the story you tell about your first board meeting, everything you do or say promotes an image of who you are and how you'll be on the job. So make sure it's a positive one. Choose to focus on what you have to offer the company rather than on what you don't. Choose to smile when the interviewer is obviously making light of something. Choose to move the conversation forward by offering a specific example of a time you wowed your supervisor. And if she asks if you found the office without any trouble, by all means *choose to answer yes.* (Because you basically did, didn't you? You're here.) Skip the equally true comment about how hard it was to locate the doorbell. Or how MapQuest got the street name wrong. Or how traffic . . . 'nuff said. Promote a positive connection and you'll be miles ahead of the competition.

And there's no need to stop there. In addition to engaging, thinking, assessing and promoting, you could also:

- *Solve* a company problem

- *Convince* the employer that you will be an asset to the company

- *Win* the employer's confidence

- *Identify* a need for your expertise

- *Facilitate* interesting discussion

- *Overcome* objections

- *Gather* information about the position

- *Demonstrate* your potential value

Those are some examples to jog your imagination. Being active in the interview is basically about maintaining an appropriately active mind-set. So don't waste time memorizing that list. If you follow the suggestions in the rest of this book and look for opportunities to *act* rather than simply *react*, you'll find yourself doing a lot of those things naturally.

Taking an active stance in the interview will help you in innumerable ways. In addition to all the benefits we've seen so far, remaining active alleviates nervousness, because you can feel like you're the one in the driver's seat at least some of the time. You are not at the mercy of the interviewer. You give her respect and try to impress her to a certain extent, sure, but that's not the same as handing over all the power. If you come to the interview planning to engage, think, assess, promote and seize every opportunity to *do* something rather than just *be* something, you'll maximize your chances of maintaining the kind of control that makes a strong interview, from both your own point of view and the interviewer's.

The Best Answer Doesn't Have to Be the World's All-Time Best Answer

THE BEST ANSWERS share a lot of important characteristics and, by now, you're familiar with all of them. Except one. There's one more thing you absolutely need to know to give the interview of your life:

No answer has to do it all.

The questions that your interviewer will be asking you are *opportunities*—opportunities for you to show aspects of yourself that might get you hired. The good news is that, in interviews as well as life, the old saying is wrong: Opportunity actually knocks many times. If you spend your life regretting one missed opportunity, you're just not in the right frame of mind to recognize new opportunities when they present themselves. That "knocks but once" stuff is nothing but a big cop-out.

Failure to take advantage of an opportunity is not a tragedy unless you choose to turn it into one. It can be remedied very simply, by taking advantage of the next one that comes along. Nowhere is this principle more evident than in the series of opportunities known as the job interview.

There are plenty of people out there like Larissa. She thinks if she doesn't get the job of her dreams her life will be over. She's fresh out of college and has always idolized Bill Gates. It's Microsoft or bust. Her interviewer at this venerable company asks her if she's always liked computers and Larissa says, "Yes. Absolutely. So much."

And then Larissa sits and stares and wants to kill herself. Her nerves have gotten the best of her. She's given a stupid, too-short, substanceless answer and is sure she sees in the interviewer's eyes that she's been written off. The interview may as well be over. Larissa is imagining the phone call she'll make to her boyfriend, telling him she's going to have to move back in with her parents and find a minimum wage job somewhere.

Larissa has made two big mistakes—actually the same mistake twice. Her big mistake is *not* in giving a short, substanceless answer. That's simply a failure to take advantage of an opportunity, which is not the end of the world. If she didn't blow it out of proportion, she would be able to go on to give more substantive answers to future questions, and that first answer would all but disappear from the interviewer's impression of her. Larissa's big mistake, to use another old adage, is that she put all her eggs in the same basket, first by deciding that Microsoft was the only place she could possibly work, and second by imagining that her answer to the first question had to carry dozens of interview eggs all by itself.

No possible answer—no matter how weak or unhelpful—is ever as big a mistake as this mistake in *attitude*. Because you can always recover from an answer, but a bad attitude will defeat you every time.

First of all, just as there's no such thing as the Perfect Employee, there's no such thing as the Perfect Job. Ultimately any job will be what you make of it, and it's just possible that Larissa might end up very

happy working at Apple, appalling as that idea might seem to her at
first. The job at Microsoft just can't be all that she's cracked it up to be.
There's nothing wrong with really wanting a particular job, of course,
but an all-or-nothing attitude is generally based in some kind of illu-
sion, and it's a trap you don't want to fall into.

This is not to suggest that jobs are easy to come by and that
everybody will have lots of offers to choose from. A job search can be a
difficult time in a person's life, but no matter how much it seems as
though a particular interview is your last hope, it isn't. You'll want to do
your absolute best to get the job, naturally, but your absolute best won't
be accessible to you if you're constantly worried about slipping up because you imagine this job is the only way you will ever get food on the
table. You want to make the most of the *opportunity*, but if you scare
yourself into thinking that this is opportunity's one and only knock,
you're sure to scare yourself out of doing well in the interview.

On a smaller scale, the same thing can happen in answering individual questions. What matters in an interview performance is the
overall impression you make on the interviewer. Larissa's overall impression may not be good after her first answer, but she has a lot more
answers to give, which add up to a big opportunity to tip the scales
from "stupid and substanceless" to "the right one for the job." But not
if she can't (or won't put in the necessary effort to) recover emotionally
from the embarrassment of one "bad" answer. You have to remind
yourself to keep sight of the big picture, which is never as black as an
individual splotch can make it seem.

Using Your Training to Best Advantage

You do not have to do everything this book tells you to do. As we've
stressed over and over, the interview is a totally subjective experience,

different for everyone, and you can only succeed by doing it in a way that is shaped by your own uniqueness.

If you try to give answers that are in no way shaped by who you are, you are likely to fail. And you will be similarly likely to fail if you allow all your answers to be too short or too long or too passive, or if you otherwise systematically ignore the characteristics of good interview answers that these pages have described.

But you don't have to do it all. An interview that never includes a single developed story is not necessarily a bad interview. If that interview includes lots of short, concrete examples of excellent traits and skills, they may well make up for the lack of an anecdote. If you tend to ramble, but your rambling includes lots of intersections of your abilities with specific needs of the company, your rambling may not be held against you.

You now have a set of simple and effective tools to apply to your interview tasks. Which means that if you find yourself up a creek, you know you have a paddle. The tools work for *any* question, so they give you a way to assess how the interview is going, and several ways to correct for any errors you think you've committed along the way.

The point of having several tools at your disposal is to take the pressure off, rather than ratchet it up. Don't go into your interview planning to display all the best characteristics of the best answers on every question. Go in armed with the right attitude: There are no right or wrong answers, and you're prepared to handle anything.

PART 4

A Never-Fail Process

BY THIS POINT IN THE BOOK, you should have a clear sense of what is important in a job interview and what is not. Simply put, your own authenticity and uniqueness matter; everything else doesn't.

Trust it. *You* are all you have to work with, but that's enough. You have what it takes to get this job. (If you don't, why are you wasting your valuable time at the interview, anyway?)

But you also realize that making the employer see you as the right one for the job is not necessarily an easy task. It doesn't take sleight of hand or any kind of mysterious insider know-how. But it does take bravery, preparation and an act of will. And it's much easier if you have a clear plan—not, of course, a set of sound bytes you're prepared to spout off, but simply a solid understanding of how you're going to proceed once you walk into that room.

Now that you're familiar with the basic characteristics of good answers, how will you use this knowledge to answer the first question when you're actually face-to-face with the interviewer? Well, you obviously don't know what words you'll say, because you don't even know yet what the question will be. But *how* you're going to answer a question is not at all the same as *what* answer you're going to give. The *how* is all about the way you *approach the task* of answering it. In other words, what is your *process* going to be?

While the answers to individual questions will all be different, a reliable process will apply to any question that can possibly be asked. So a reliable process will keep you grounded throughout the interview. If you start answering questions without giving some thought to what your process is, you may leave yourself open to nerves, distractions and unhelpful habits, like rambling. A step-by-step procedure will keep you focused on what's important and ensure that you maximize each opportunity to show yourself in the best possible light.

As with any good system, simple is best. So here it is. This is the best way to answer 1,000,001 interview questions.

A Never-Fail Process

1. Listen to the question.
2. Think about why you're glad to be asked that question.
3. Identify the interviewer's need in asking that question.
4. Say something that shows how you can fill that need.
5. Give a relevant illustration from your life.
6. Stop, relax and breathe.
7. Listen to the next question.

This process is simple to state, but not necessarily as easy to carry out. You'll need to really know what each step is and why you're doing it.

And you'll need to really believe in it and fully embrace the appropriate mind-set. But if you trust yourself and your preparation, and practice a little bit, it will work every time. Here are the steps in more detail:

1) Listen to the question.

Well, of course. Who wouldn't listen to the question? But the trick is to listen *well*! That's what most people don't do. Instead they get distracted by a jackhammer outside the window or the thumping of their own pulse or the inadequacy of the answer they just gave, or they get cocky and jump to conclusions about the rest of what the interviewer is going to say, or they devote too much energy to planning their answer while the interviewer is still asking the question.

Listening seems like something that happens naturally but, of course, that kind of passive "listening" is really nothing more than *hearing*, which we all know is a different thing altogether. Effective listening—true listening—is an active process of taking in and digesting what you're hearing. It involves the thinking parts of the brain, not just the bones of the inner ear. Unfortunately, the stress of a situation like a job interview can somewhat numb those cerebral areas if you let it, and then you may find yourself on autopilot, content to let the inner ear vibrate away. If that happens, you'll probably hear enough to get by, but you won't have taken in enough detail—about the precise wording, the attitude, the tone of voice—to craft an answer that will really nail the question.

You avoid autopilot—and the accompanying sense of flying through a fog—by understanding that your periods of listening must be just as active as your periods of answering. True listening is not about taking turns—*she says something, then I say something, then she says something*—it's about facilitating a lively exchange of information.

So how do you do that?

Think, look and reflect.

Think: Analyze while you listen.

- Work to be sure you're completely clear about what is being asked. You need to actively connect the pieces of the question into a cohesive whole, even if the interviewer seems to be rambling. (It happens.)

- What can you tell from the tone of voice? (Does she seem to be enthusiastically piggybacking on your previous answer, or struggling to come up with something new to say? How might that information help you communicate with her better?)

- At the same time, be thinking ahead to how you might want to answer. Don't think so far ahead that you stop paying attention! But, especially if the question is long or complicated, you should use the time to take note of how what the interviewer is saying relates to you. Don't be afraid of interpreting the question in a way that makes it easy for you to answer.

Look: Maintain strong eye contact.

- Energetic, thoughtful eye contact will allow you to pick up more clues about the interviewer's precise meaning and attitude, and will ultimately make you more comfortable relating to her as another human being.

- Eye contact will keep you focused on the interviewer and what she's saying, helping you avoid any distractions that may arise.

- Besides actually helping you listen well, good eye contact strengthens the *impression* that you're listening well, which is something any interviewer likes to see.

Reflect: Let the interviewer know you're with her.

- Find ways, in addition to eye contact, to let the interviewer know that you're paying attention and understanding exactly what she's saying. An occasional nod or smile can do wonders to strengthen the relationship. (Don't overdo it, though!)

- It's perfectly fine to ask for clarification, as long as you do so politely. ("Are you wondering specifically about my last job, or my career as a whole?")

- If you're really listening well, you'll be prepared to reflect some of the question back in your answer, to show that you understand and care about the specifics of what she's asking. ("When you mentioned 'office politics' that made me think of the time when . . .")

This kind of proper, active listening is one of your most valuable tools for setting yourself off from the rest of the crowd. While they're glazing over and nodding distractedly, you'll be nodding for all the right reasons.

2) Think about why you're glad to be asked that question.

After you've listened carefully to a question, don't answer immediately. It's okay (even good) to take a breath. It's also okay and good to take a moment to think. Remember not to take too long, but that moment is important, and what you choose to think about in that brief time is crucial.

An awful lot of job interview candidates spend that time worrying that the question is somehow bad news. They seem to think that the reason an interviewer asks you questions is because he's trying to weed you out. Question after unrelenting question, he chips away at your façade, trying to uncover your weaknesses, to prove you're not really who and what you say you are, to get you to trip up and make a fool of yourself, so he can get you out of there and get on to the next interview, perhaps after a short break for a cup of tea with the devil.

But by now you're through with worrying about worst case scenarios, right? You're focusing on what's probable and what's productive. That means you're ready to fight the human tendency to be afraid of the questions.

Make this a conscious step of your interviewing process so you don't forget it. When the interviewer asks, "Why did you leave your last job?" *refuse* to assume he thinks your last boss hated you. That kind of knee-jerk, defensive response is nothing more than some very unpleasant, unhealthy, unproductive psychology trying to get in your way from inside your own head.

Instead, take a quick moment after each question—a second or two—to think about *why that question is good news for you*. You're in charge; you make up the reason.

"Why did you leave your last job?"

Think: *Ah! I'm glad you asked that, because now I can tell you about my lifelong ambition to manage an enthusiastic team.*
Or: *Ah! I'm glad you asked that, because now I can tell you about how much happier I am now that I live here in San Francisco.*

Or, worst-case scenario, if you've been fired from your last job for substandard performance:

Ah! I'm glad you asked that, because this gives me an opportunity to explain why I am much better suited for this position than for my last one.

Or: whatever. Interpret the question positively, believably and in a way that will allow you to take full advantage of the opportunity the question presents.

If you haven't guessed yet, you can (and should) do this for *every question*. Choosing to be happy about the questions is a crucial aspect of thinking positively, and it will open up your mind to all sorts of great answers that a defensive attitude will make inaccessible.

3) Identify the interviewer's need in asking that question.

So you've interpreted the question positively from your own point of view. But don't forget to keep in mind the *interviewer's* point of view, too, so you'll be prepared to match what you have to say to the kinds of things he needs to hear.

Think again about, "Why did you leave your last job?" If your tendency is to think he's trying to get some dirt on you—grow up! Remember that he wants nothing more than for you to show him you're the strong, positive, confident person he's looking for. So think productively. Maybe he wants to know why you want to work for him. Maybe he wants assurance that you plan on sticking around for a while. Maybe he wants to know a little bit more about who you are and what makes you tick. And he's offering you an opportunity to tell him.

Please remember that you can't be expected to read his mind. There are any number of needs that might be operating, probably several at once, that you could satisfy. So pick one. If it turns out he needs something different from what you gave him, trust that he'll ask another question.

"Where do you hope to be in five years?" If you're not sure, don't focus on how unsure you are. He doesn't want to prove that you haven't given this question enough thought, or that you're too ambitious for his taste, or not ambitious enough. Even if he is a poor enough interviewer to have some ideal answer in his head that he's waiting for you to hit or miss, it's certainly not your responsibility to try to figure out what that might be. He's offered an opportunity for you to talk about your hopes and dreams, or your ideas of how you could grow into the position you're applying for, or what books you hope someday to read, or . . . any future-oriented thoughts about yourself that you think might help him understand you well enough to see you as the person he's looking for. Make a conscious decision that those are exactly the kinds of things he's fishing for.

Notice how much more control you'll have with this approach. Refuse to believe anyone who claims you should *know* what the proper interpretation of any given question is; that's a totalitarian outlook that closes off possibilities rather than opening them up. Instead, go in there with the understanding that you get to *decide* what need you think the interviewer is trying to fulfill with each question. It's *your* interpretation that matters. You maintain control by consciously choosing to assign positive and productive motives to the interviewer, no matter what destructive thoughts your inner whiner tries to throw in your way.

4) Say something that shows how you can fill that need.

Remember, you've come to this interview well prepared. (If it helps you to think competitively, note that most of the other candidates will not have anywhere near the kind of preparation you've acquired just by reading this book.)

So here you are across from the interviewer. You've listened carefully to a question, given yourself a reason to be happy the question was asked, decided what need might have led the interviewer to ask the question and now it's time to speak. What do you say?

If you've thought at least a little bit about your qualities and the requirements of the job, the answer will be there waiting for you. This is the central idea you must take to heart. No one can tell you what to say, but no one has to. It's not about knowing the words ahead of time, but about following the right thought processes along the way. You've done that, so you're fine. You have things you want to say, and you have someone who wants to hear them.

So this is what you do: You answer the question by showing how you can meet the interviewer's need.

Sarah walks into an office building and shakes hands comfortably and confidently with the gentleman who will be conducting her job interview. She's a little nervous, but she's well prepared, so she feels in control. (She's read this book.)

After a little chitchat, the interviewer asks the first real question, that old chestnut, "Where do you want to be in five years?" Someone who's done less preparing might freeze up or say something stupid like, "That's a good question!" Sarah, however, applies step two of the process and immediately recognizes that she's happy that question was asked—because it provides a great opportunity for her to talk about the course of study in computer skills she's just undertaken. She might have come up with any number of other reasons, but that's the one that occurs to her. She doesn't worry that it's not the best choice, because she knows worrying is counterproductive. She runs with it.

Sarah's next step is to decide why the interviewer might have asked that question. She decides that part of his intention might be to determine how committed she'll be to furthering the goals of his company if he hires her. She finds that she's smiling, and this is what comes out of her mouth:

"I'm somebody who always likes to be learning something, and I've recently started taking classes in computer technology. In five years I can see myself using computers to turn this position into something even more important and productive than it is now, or maybe advancing into a new position with more technological responsibilities."

That answer does not hedge Sarah's bets against every possible eventuality, but that's not her job. If the interviewer was hoping for something that sounded more ambitious, or less ambitious, or more like Sarah liked him so much that she'd want to still be working closely with him personally five years from now—oh well. She's given an answer that is truthful, covers a lot of ground, shows an understanding of what seems to be important to the company (and hence to the interviewer), shows positive thinking, makes good use of her trait of being an ongoing learner and is specifically responsive to the question that was asked. That's a good answer. And Sarah arrived at it by maintaining her focus on what's important, trusting herself and following a thought process that is simple and reliable.

And the best news is, that was only one of hundreds of answers Sarah could have given. You don't give *the* answer, you give *an* answer, one of the innumerable strong answers you're capable of constructing, and you get to choose which one.

5) Give a relevant illustration from your life.

Remember that a good answer is not too short. You've come to the interview armed with examples of your good qualities in action and a few stories that paint a picture of what you're like in a real work situation. All you have to do is remember to use them. And you treat every question as an opportunity. That's how you exploit your uniqueness by turning generic answers into answers that only you could possibly give.

In most cases it will be easy to back your answer up with an example, because your sense of what you're like comes from your memory of things you've done. Why did Bill just tell the interviewer that he's a fast decision maker? Well, okay, maybe he said it because he thought that's what she wanted to hear, when in fact he's not a fast decision maker at all. In that case, Bill has fallen into one of the big traps that we're trying to save you from (he should go back and re-read "The Best Answer Is

Truthful"!). So instead of trying to pull him out of some hole he's dug for himself, let's assume instead that it's true: Bill is, in fact, a fast decision maker. If he said it because it's true, that means he's remembering times when he made fast decisions. He's ready to say, "A couple years ago we had designed a deck for a client who suddenly decided she needed it a week ahead of time for her parents' surprise fortieth anniversary party. I spent an hour with the contractor telling him which plans to scale back and which ones not to, and it got done on time and the client loved it."

Not every question will lend itself to an example, and that's okay. But always be on the lookout for opportunities to provide concrete evidence of your rightness for the job. If you don't make it part of your conscious process to look for an example on every question, then you're going to miss a lot of opportunities.

For example, the question of where you hope to be in five years may not seem to lend itself to the technique of illustration. But if you're on the lookout for opportunities, you might come up with something like this:

"In my last job I set myself a goal of becoming a team leader within a year, and I achieved it with the help of a lot of books on managerial psychology. So my system of meeting goals by educating myself has worked for me in the past."

If you're remembering to look for examples, something like that just might occur to you, and it's going to give a great boost to your answer.

Once again, please remember: If the above answers sound contrived, that's because they are. They've been contrived by us, as *hypothetical* examples of winning qualities. Your own examples won't sound the least bit contrived, because they'll be *real*. That's what you've spent the rest of this book working on: real, vivid, one-of-a-kind pictures of who you are and what you can do for this employer.

6) Stop, relax and breathe.

Remember that even remembering to stop may not be as obvious as it seems. You must *choose* to end your answer, instead of letting it die a slow death. No single answer should be expected to tell the whole story, right? Don't let yourself ramble on in an attempt to cover all the bases. Too long is as bad as too short. If you've spoken honestly to what you perceive as the interviewer's need and provided an example, that's a good answer. End it, so the interviewer can move on.

In some cases the interviewer's response—a puzzled look, say— may suggest that some clarification or expansion of your answer would be a good thing. That's fine. Go ahead and clarify or expand—a little. But second-guessing yourself and overelaborating are anything but productive.

In the short moment of finishing an answer and preparing for the next question, consciously choose to relax. Physical tension may have built up in your body in the course of your answer without you realizing it. Take a deep breath and let it out.

7) Listen to the next question.

Maintain your concentration and your positive attitude, and repeat the process.

And that's it. This process will keep you grounded and focused. It will ensure that you will be in control, and it will help you maintain the right attitude throughout the interview. You've come there for the opportunity to answer questions, and the interviewer has kindly asked you some! And you have a process for approaching each and every one of them.

If you worry that the process is too rigid and will cramp your style, just don't let it. The process leaves plenty of room for variation and improvisation as the mood strikes, so you should feel grounded and yet free. If you skip a step now and then, who cares? Just don't skip the same one too many times, or you'll pay for your feeling of spontaneity by weakening your overall presentation.

And, most important, understand that the thought processes involved happens in a split second. The communication we are describing only seems complex because, in breaking it down step-by-step, you are forced to make it overly conscious, at least at first. Soon, though, you'll get used to doing it all automatically. (Remember how hyperconscious you were when you first learned to drive? Now you probably hardly give a thought to the mechanics of this highly complicated life-or-death activity!) So, as you prepare for your interview, find as many opportunities as you can (dinners with friends, cocktail parties, blind dates, bedtime chats with the kids) to practice these skills until they become, if not first, then at least second nature.

An Interview Case Study:
Lisa B.

This fictional job search scenario gives an example of a strong preparation regimen and illustrates the strength and flexibility of the Never-Fail Process in producing terrific answers to a wide variety of questions.

THE JOB ANNOUNCEMENT

Happy Trails, a leader in the development of active adult communities, has an immediate opening for the position of Activities Director. Must possess an outgoing and exciting personality, and be an energetic self-starter. Experience in financial management, recreation and personnel management required.

THE CANDIDATE

Name   Lisa B.

Education   Graduated 14 years ago from University of Arizona, History major, Music minor

Employment • 3 years as Assistant to the Director of Audience
   History   Development at the Arizona Symphony

            • 6 years as Director of Community Outreach at Arizona Sym-
              phony, in charge of bringing programs to area schools and
              attracting new and diverse populations to orchestra perform-
              ances

            • 2 years as talent agent representing musical groups and other
              acts who performed at local clubs, weddings and special
              events

            • 3 years as full-time mom

   Hobbies   Tennis, running and knitting

Three years ago, Lisa had a son and left her job with the orchestra
but continued to book the occasional gig for a client of her talent
agency. Her son began preschool last month and she is ready to return
to the workforce full-time.

Lisa comes across the Happy Trails ad and, even though she has no
direct experience working with senior communities, she faxes her
cover letter and résumé. To her surprise and delight, she is called in for
an interview the very next day with a Mr. Baxter.

Note that "financial management, recreation and personnel
management"—the three requirements specified in the job
announcement—do not jump out as major features of Lisa's employment history, at least on paper. But luckily her résumé was enough to
get her in the door, so she's going to have a chance to impress an interviewer. Lisa feels confident that this is a job she would enjoy and be
good at, so she proceeds to build her case. She starts by finding out
more about Happy Trails.

THE COMPANY

From company website

> "Happy Trails is a premier retirement destination for active adults, ages 55 and older. Each community features spectacular homes, championship golf, hiking, tennis, swimming, fitness, live entertainment and volunteer pursuits. These activities are the building blocks for new friendships and camaraderie with people just like you. Come find out how full life at Happy Trails can be."

From Hoover's Online company information site

> Happy Trails is a planned community with more than 1,000 residents (growing larger by the day) and boasts a full-time staff of nearly 80. The community features homes that range in price from about $140,000 to $350,000. Amenities include more than fifteen chartered clubs to nurture interests from aviation and bridge to computers and gardening in addition to the activities listed on the company website. Mr. Baxter, Lisa's interviewer, is the V.P. of Operations for Happy Trails.

From salary.com

> The typical salary range for similar positions in Phoenix, Arizona is $38,000 - $52,000.

From Lisa's mother, who has a friend living in a similar community in New Mexico

> The residents are likely to be extremely fit, well educated and independent—not at all interested in bingo and other activities traditionally associated with senior living. Many probably moved in as couples but have lost a spouse over time and have continued to live in the community as a widowed person.

There's a lot of delicious Swiss cheese here, but at first all Lisa can see is the holes. She worked with volunteers when she was director of community outreach at the symphony, but didn't really have a staff, so she can't claim to have lots of experience as a supervisor. The only bookkeeping she ever really did was whatever was necessary to keep things on track at her one-person talent agency. And, most glaring of all, she has no professional experience with seniors.

She did always wish her grandfather had been able to enjoy the benefits of a place like Happy Trails, though, rather than living out his life as a sad and lonely widower. And most of her ushers at the symphony had always been seniors, and they were so enthusiastic and good at the job that she often gave them extra duties, which they appreciated.

Continuing to brainstorm for intersections between her experiences and the needs of the company, Lisa eventually comes up with something like the following chart:

Happy Trails needs:	Lisa is:	As demonstrated by:
someone who can take initiative (a "self-starter")	exactly that	her creation of a successful talent agency from scratch
someone who projects enthusiasm ("outgoing . . . exciting . . . energetic")	outgoing, exciting and energetic	the personality that she will display in the interview, and "The Bar Mitzvah Story" (see page 109)
someone who can manage a budget ("experience in financial management")	competent in that area	her successful handling of her own budgeting and bookkeeping as a talent agent (albeit on a small scale)

Happy Trails needs:	Lisa is:	As demonstrated by:
someone who can manage and motivate a support staff ("experience in personnel management")	sure she would be good at that (although her direct experience is limited)	her supervision of symphony ushers and coordination of many event participants at a time
someone who can start right away	ready	her availability and enthusiasm
someone with experience in leisure programming (or "recreation")	experienced in arts programming and able and willing to learn about the rest	her success booking talent for events, her passion for her own hobbies, and her willingness to take on new challenges with the symphony
someone who can coordinate events that appeal to a wide range of interests	experienced in coordinating events for diverse populations	her work developing different outreach programs for different schools
someone who appreciates the sophisticated tastes of the residents	well-connected to the arts community	the ease with which she has attracted the area's top artists to perform at events she has coordinated for the symphony and through her talent business
someone whose role can expand along with the population of Happy Trails	always ready to take on new challenges	her ascent through the ranks of the symphony
someone who can help new residents facilitate friendships	very good at developing community	her implementation of "community nights" at the symphony, which encouraged audience members to get to know one another

Happy Trails needs:	Lisa is:	As demonstrated by:
someone who can develop activities for singles as well as couples	sensitive to issues of isolation and loneliness	her feelings about her grandfather
someone who works well with upper management	easy to work with and very loyal	the trust that her employers placed in her as she took on more and more challenging roles at the symphony and the unusual length of time (nine years) that she worked there
someone who will get along with the senior population	well-liked and easy to get along with	her good relationships with symphony volunteers (many of whom were seniors) and her ability to develop positive relationships with difficult symphony subscribers (see story page 113)

In the interview, Lisa will concentrate not on those areas where the company's needs do not exactly match up with what she has to offer, but on the strongest intersections of her strengths with the company's needs.

Lisa now has everything she needs to effectively interview for this position, no matter what her interviewer turns out to be like and no matter what questions he asks. By following the steps outlined in the last chapter, she's sure to give her best possible interview, no matter what the circumstances.

As an illustration of the variety of situations Lisa is now prepared for, here are excerpts from a few of the millions of strong interview performances she might find herself delivering tomorrow.

Note that these are not the *right* answers. They are simply *her* answers. But, you see, Lisa, though imaginary, has clearly digested the lessons of this book. Her answers are generated by the Never-Fail Process presented in the last chapter, they exhibit the best-answer characteristics and they're answers that only Lisa, using the specific details of her life as outlined above, could possibly give. Which is why they work so well.

INTERVIEW SCENARIO #1

Mr. Baxter turns out to be an affable guy in his fifties, with a slightly disheveled appearance. He makes a lot of direct eye contact and laughs easily. He welcomes Lisa with a warm handshake and, after engaging her in a bit of small talk, proceeds to more substantive matters.

Interviewer: I see you've spent many years in the music business. Why do you want to make the switch to a job in the recreation field?

Possible response

So much of what I enjoyed about both my work with the symphony and as a talent agent was trying to develop events that would be especially interesting to the people we were trying to reach, and I love the idea of having that as a daily challenge at Happy Trails. As outreach director at the symphony, I prepared programs for schools with strong music departments where the students couldn't wait to meet the orchestra conductor, and also for schools where most of the kids had never been exposed to classical music of any kind. Here at Happy Trails, I would enjoy developing programs that give residents something they already love and also exposing them to new things to get excited about.

Why it works

It's specific (not too short or too long) and makes a positive statement about how Lisa would use her experiences and values to benefit the company (in other words, it's active).

Or maybe she chooses a different approach:

Possible response

My interest in this position is actually a direct out-growth of my work in the music field. I've been lucky enough to see how fully the arts enrich people's lives, and I would be thrilled to have a job that allowed me to bring all kinds of arts, entertainment and other recreational opportunities to people on a daily basis.

Why it works

It's truthful, paints a picture of Lisa as a caring, passionate person and gives a strong explanation of why she wants the job (answering a possible question behind the question).

Interviewer: The residents of Happy Trails are a surprisingly diverse group. When you talk about activities and recreation, what do you imagine planning for them?

Possible response

Yes, I noticed on your website that the residents have a lot of different interests and very sophisticated tastes. I think that I would first want to know which activities have been the most successful over the past few years and which have fallen by the wayside. I would also want to make sure that there was something to appeal to everyone, whether their interests run toward sports or more to the visual arts, whether they like to drive or to walk, whether they're living with someone or by themselves. Has Happy Trails done any recent surveys of people's interests?

Why it works

It demonstrates her knowledge of the company and the community in a gracious way. Also, Lisa's answer presents a methodology for deepening her understanding of the needs of the community she would be working for, illustrating her unique combination of curiosity and practicality.

Or

Possible response

I noticed that your charter clubs cater to a lot of interests, particularly in the area of sports and leisure, which is great. And I also saw that you have a large community room in your town center complex. One thing that I think I could offer would be to bring in unique entertainment opportunities from some of the area's top performers. At the symphony we al-

Why it works

It offers a very specific opportunity based on Lisa's unique past experience. This is a great example of how to be active in an interview.

ways had great success with "Meet the Artist" nights—an evening of entertainment followed by a brief discussion and reception. Do you think that kind of event might be of interest to the residents?

Interviewer: The position carries with it a lot of responsibility. How comfortable are you with that?

Possible response	Why it works
I like to work in an exciting environment where I have a lot of responsibility. As director of community out-reach for the symphony, I was in charge of coordinating lots of high-visibility events with major performers on tight schedules. I learned if you stay calm at the helm (and have a good backup plan), things will usually turn out all right.	It speaks directly to an implied question behind the question ("How well do you handle pressure?"). Also, it's succinct and paints a picture of Lisa as a calm, clear thinker.

Or she could use this opportunity to go even deeper:

Possible response	Why it works
I'm very comfortable with responsibility and handling the pressure that comes along with it. When I ran my own talent business, I frequently booked entertain-ment for people's most important life events—weddings, major corporate affairs, things like that. And I knew how important it was to these people that the events go well. I remember one particularly crazy experience in the early days of my business when one of my bands got a flat tire on the way to a bar mitzvah. I was there to help with the setup and, seeing that the kids were ready for some entertain-ment but no band was in sight, I stepped up to the mike and just started an impromptu, pop-culture trivia contest. I don't know what made me think of it, but it really worked. The kids starting screaming out answers, going nuts for the silly prizes I was handing out (someone went home with the table centerpiece) and just having the best time. Ultimately the band did	It provides vivid examples of many of Lisa's unique qualities: her resourceful-ness, her grace under pressure, her outgoing nature and her sense of humor. It also clearly speaks to another possi-ble question behind the question: "Are you able to assume levels of respon-sibility beyond the basic requirements of the job?" *Note that she couldn't answer every question with a story as elaborate as this, but one or two over the*

show up and was great (thank goodness I didn't have to sing "Hava Nagilah" a cappella!), but I learned that sometimes even the best-laid plans will go awry, and you have to be willing to do something a little different to give people the kind of experience they deserve.

course of the interview would really give the flavor of who she is.

Interviewer: The activities director is responsible for managing an annual budget of approximately $300,000 a year. Do you have any experience with that kind of thing?

Possible response

Yes, I do. I created my own budget and did all the bookkeeping and reporting for my talent agency, which operated in the black every year of its existence.

Why it works

It's truthful, to the point and positive (doesn't call attention to the fact that her company's annual budget was much smaller).

Or

Possible response

I have some experience with financial management because I created my own company several years ago. I know quite a bit about QuickBooks accounting software and am a pretty quick study when it comes to other kinds of programming.

Why it works

It's active (introduces new information), and demonstrates her desire to learn new things.

INTERVIEW SCENARIO #2

Mr. Baxter is a fast-talking fidgeter. He plays with a paper clip on his desk during Lisa's answers. The following exchange occurs midway through her interview.

Interviewer: Am I missing something on your résumé or have you never worked in recreation?

Possible response

It's true that I've never had a formal job in recreation, but I'm not a stranger to the field. My work with the symphony and my own talent business have given me a great deal of experience planning many different kinds of arts events. So when it comes to music and entertainment programming I feel very confident. As far as sports and other kinds of recreational programming go, I'm a fast learner. In fact, when I was promoted to outreach director at the symphony I had no formal outreach experience but I contacted colleagues in the field and gave myself a crash course. I would expect to do the same kind of research at this job, finding out what the residents want and how to most effectively facilitate that.

Why it works

It's truthful, stays positive, avoids defensiveness, highlights transferable skills and demonstrates ability to "self-start."

But this might work just as well:

Possible response

You're right—I've never worked directly in recreation although I have spent most of my career in the arts and entertainment field, where there's a lot of crossover. I'm also very passionate about my own recreational activities—I play tennis, knit, and I've even run a marathon—so I can appreciate how important it is to have a wide variety of well-developed activities that meet a range of interests. I'm very excited about the possibility of working in a position that combines both my career and my personal interests.

Why it works

It is uniquely Lisa's (how many people have run a marathon?) and paints a picture of her as a passionate and motivated person.

Interviewer: Are you good with people?

Possible response

I would have to say that I'm very good with people. I think this is one of the main reasons I'm drawn to Happy Trails—because there's lots of daily contact with the people that you're planning the events for. One of the most gratifying aspects of my work with the symphony was the relationships I developed with the long-term subscribers. It was fun thinking up

Why it works

It takes a vague, lazy question and focuses it in a productive, professional direction. It's also active and not too short.

which special guests would appeal to which people. I
even developed "community nights" where
subscribers could attend a reception and get to
know one another better. Some people who had
been single subscribers for years began attending
performances together as a result of those events. It
was incredibly gratifying to see friendships grow out
of common interests.

Or maybe this:

Possible response	Why it works
I would have to say that I'm very good with people. I've always been someone who found it easy to talk with people—even people I've just met at a cocktail party. I think it's because I am genuinely interested in learning what people are interested in, how they think, what's important to them. If you ask questions, people really tend to open up. This is one of the things I would most look forward to as activities director here—the chance to get to know the residents and participate in the community life here.	It promotes a positive image of her and it high-lights her enthusiastic, outgoing, energetic nature.

Interviewer: Our residents have high expectations for the quality of
the programming. Some of them are quite vocal, in fact. How would
you handle that?

Possible response	Why it works
Oh, I know people can be challenging sometimes, but I don't mind that.	It doesn't, actually. (But we already said not everything has to be the world's all-time best answer. She'll have other chances.)

Or

Possible response

Well, I think it's good that there's an expectation that the activities at Happy Trails will be top-notch. And I would hope that residents would feel comfortable coming to me and voicing their desires and concerns. My work in the audience development department of the symphony gave me an up-close-and-personal relationship with symphony subscribers, who were incredibly interesting people although not always the easiest group to satisfy. I remember one gentleman who booked his subscription a little later than usual and he was furious when his favorite seats were not available for a particular performance. He was ranting on the phone and, instead of getting defensive with him, I just invited him to be my personal guest at the next Sunday discussion event. Never mind that the discussion was free and open to the public—he thought it was a major perk and he later became a big donor to the orchestra! And I actually really enjoyed the time I spent with him. I think when you communicate with respect and openness, people really appreciate it, and it makes your job a lot more fun, too.

Why it works

It's a vivid story that gets right to the heart of an unspoken question ("How will you deal with complaints?"). It demonstrates a uniquely positive outlook, and illustrates both Lisa's excellent people skills and her problem-solving abilities. It also makes great use of a story that Lisa prepared not for this or any particular question, but because of its flexibility.

INTERVIEW SCENARIO #3

Mr. Baxter is a quiet, almost somber middle-aged gentleman. He pauses frequently between thoughts. He concludes the interview with the following questions.

Interviewer: What salary were you hoping for?

Possible response

Did you have a salary range in mind?

Why it works

It's active (questions always are) and definitely not too long.

Or, a little more out on a limb:

Possible response

At the symphony, my salary was in the upper forties and I'm looking for something comparable.

Why it works

It's truthful and demonstrates her knowledge of the company, the position and the field.

Interviewer: Do you have experience working with seniors?

Possible response

My experience working with seniors has mostly been managing volunteer ushers at the symphony, the majority of whom were people over fifty-five. What I remember most about that was how enthusiastic they were about both the symphony and their volunteer duties. In fact, I even ended up hiring a volunteer usher who was in her late sixties or early seventies as a summer replacement for one of my outreach assistants one year. She was absolutely terrific and it was a great lesson for me in appreciating how vital people can be at that age. I was so pleased to see that Happy Trails has so many opportunities for residents to volunteer. That's a really strong interest of mine.

Why it works

It's truthful without being apologetic for her lack of experience and it makes a strong statement about her values.

Or

Possible response

I don't have a lot of professional experience working with seniors, although I did manage our ushers program at the symphony, which consisted mainly of senior citizens, who were great. But, it's funny; I think the fact that this is a senior community is exactly what draws me to this position. I was always very close to my grandparents, both of whom were terrifically active people up into their eighties. But when my grandmother died, my grandfather just stopped pursuing his passions. He didn't play golf anymore or go fishing or have his weekly bridge night. He just

Why it works

It's very unique and personal (in an appropriate way), and it speaks to an important question behind the question ("Why do you want a job in a senior community if you've never worked with seniors?").

gave in to his depression and isolation and, in spite of his physical health, ended up in an assisted living facility where he eventually died. It was incredibly sad. And I can't help but think how much better it would have been for him to have lived at a place like Happy Trails. For me, the idea of being able to contribute to a community like this is really an amazing opportunity.

Interviewer: What questions do you have for me?

Possible response

When were you hoping someone could start?

Why it works

It provides an opportunity for her to express her interest in starting right away.

Or

Possible response

What are the specific responsibilities of the activities director with respect to personnel management?

Why it works

It's important information for her to know and it hasn't come up.

Or

Possible response

Anything she is genuinely interested in.

Why it works

It's an opportunity to further the conversation and make a more informed decision about whether this is the right job for her.

Lessons from Lisa

No matter which of the above scenarios you consider, Lisa B. barely wasted a moment in this interview. She consistently took advantage of—and often created—opportunities to make the employer see her in the job. She seemed genuinely pleased that each question was asked. Even when faced with less-than-stellar interviewers, she was ready and able to move the conversation forward.

Her success in the interview came from her ability to be herself—her confident, outgoing, interested, interesting self—even in the midst of one of life's more artificial human interactions: a.k.a., the job interview. And, contrary to popular belief, that doesn't happen by luck (the questions weren't all easy ones) or by biology (like most of us, she's not someone who finds it easy to be cool under pressure). It happened because she prepared, and she prepared well. She made strong choices about how to communicate her potential to this particular employer. She gave thought to his needs and how she might be able to meet them. She allowed herself to take risks and to trust that what she had to offer the company was worth having. And you can't ask for any more than that. Lisa may be fictional, but we like to think she got the job.

Now it's time for you to get out there and do likewise. You won't have to answer a million and one questions on your next interview, but if you had to, you could. You know what makes an answer work and you've got the Never-Fail Process to guide the way.

In other words, you're fully prepared—to give your best answer every time.